LOUISIANA
LEGENDS & LORE

ALAN BROWN

THE
History
PRESS

Published by The History Press
Charleston, SC
www.historypress.com

Copyright © 2021 by Dr. Alan N. Brown
All rights reserved

First published 2021

Manufactured in the United States

ISBN 9781467147514

Library of Congress Control Number: 2020945779

Notice: The information in this book is true and complete to the best of our knowledge. It is offered without guarantee on the part of the author or The History Press. The author and The History Press disclaim all liability in connection with the use of this book.

CONTENTS

CONTENTS

CONTENTS

INTRODUCTION

L ouisiana is different than any other state in the union. The truth behind this rather trite pronouncement lies in its geography, its history and its culture. Named after Louis XIV, king of France from 1643 to 1715, Louisiana is composed of the uplands in the north and the alluvial region in the south, which includes the coastal marshlands and the low swamplands. Its waterways include rivers, like the Sabine and the Pearl, and countless sluggish bodies of water called bayous. Louisiana's multicultural heritage springs from its original inhabitants—the Native Americans, as well as the Spanish and French settlers who began arriving in the seventeenth century. In the early eighteenth century, slaves were transported to the state to work on plantations. Over time, all of these different nationalities intermingled to produce a patchwork of folklore, customs and superstitions that can be found nowhere else. The state's distinct culture is celebrated and preserved in its cuisine, music, religious beliefs and legends.

Folklorists began mining the state's rich treasure trove of legends in the nineteenth century. Alcee Fortier (1856–1914), a professor of folklore at Tulane University, collected Creole versions of Br'er Rabbit tales at Laura Plantation near Vacherie in the 1870s. He published these tales in *Louisiana Folk Tales: In French Dialect and English Translation, 1894*. George Washington Cable (1844–1925), who gained fame for his portrayal of Creole life in New Orleans, published a compilation of seven Louisiana legends, including the haunting of the Lalaurie House, in his book *Strange True Stories of Louisiana* (1890). Lyle Saxon (1891–1946) is arguably the greatest collector of Louisiana lore from the twentieth century. As a writer for the *Times-Picayune* in New Orleans, Saxon became fascinated with the history of the city. In 1935, when he became director of the Louisiana branch of the Federal Writers Project in Louisiana, which produced the Works Progress Administration (WPA) Guide to Louisiana, he immersed himself in the lore of the entire state. In his book *Gumbo Ya-Ya* (1945), Saxon preserved tales of pirate treasure, haunted houses, voodoo queens and cemeteries, many of which had never been written about before. Saxon clearly saw value in the folk culture that many of his contemporaries took for granted.

Louisiana Legends and Lore owes a great debt to Fortier, Cable, Saxon and all of the others who have followed their lead and sought to share Louisiana's wealth of stories with the world. The proliferation of books written about the state's unique history and culture testify to Louisiana's enduring appeal to "outsiders." As long as the people of Louisiana continue to entertain and educate themselves and the younger generations by telling the tales they grew up with, the Pelican State will remain an extremely fertile spawning ground for legends and lore.

1.

CIVIL WAR LEGENDS

THE MYSTERIOUS CONFEDERATE SUBMARINE

Baton Rouge

In 1878, a work crew was dredging Bayou St. John at the point where it joins Lake Pontchartrain, when the crew discovered what appeared to be a Civil War–era submarine. The iron vessel was twenty feet long, three feet wide and six feet deep. It was propelled by a hand crank. The crank was operated by two crew members. Historians assumed that it had been scuttled after the fall of New Orleans to keep it out of the hands of the Yankees. In 1895, the submarine was moved to Spanish Fort Amusement Park, where it was displayed as the Confederate submarine *Pioneer*. A group led by Horace Huntley built the *Pioneer* early in the war. The Confederate government established it as a privateer in May 1862. After New Orleans was captured by David Glasgow Farragut in April of that year, the Confederates scuttled the vessel in a New Orleans canal.

The submarine that was identified as the *Pioneer* was eventually neglected. By the early 1900s, it was dumped into a patch of weeds. By the time it was moved to the Camp Nicholls Confederate Home on Bayou St. John in 1908, vandals had stolen the remaining propeller blade. Part of the lower hull was missing, as well. The State Museum acquired the submarine in 1942 and displayed it in Jackson Square. A few years later, it was moved

This Confederate submarine discovered in Bayou St. John in 1878 was misidentified as the *Pioneer* for many years. *Wikimedia Commons.*

once again, this time to the Pontalba Building, where it became part of the Defense Exhibit. In 1957, the submarine was relocated to the Presbytere arcade, where it remained until 1999, when it was transport to Baton Rouge. Following a period of extensive restoration, the submarine was put on display at the Capitol Park Museum in Baton Rouge.

The submarine was displayed as the *Pioneer* until naval historian Mark Ragan found drawings of the *Pioneer* that were made by a team of Union experts. The drawings and dimensions proved that the Confederate submarine had been misidentified. The *Pioneer* was actually a cigar-shaped craft, thirty feet long and four feet wide. However, the submarine discovered in Lake Pontchartrain was a pumpkinseed-shaped vessel, twenty feet long and three feet wide. To this day, its identity is unknown.

THE LOUISIANA ORIGIN OF *DIXIE*

New Orleans

The *American Heritage Dictionary* defines the word *legend* as "an unverifiable popular story handed down from the past." Linguistic legends are the most intriguing—and tantalizing—of these mysterious tales. A good case in point is the origin of the word *Dixie*, which originally referred to the eleven Southern states that seceded from the Union between 1860 and 1861: South Carolina, Mississippi, Florida, Alabama, Georgia, Louisiana, Texas, Virginia, Arkansas, North Carolina and Tennessee. Three standard explanations have been offered for the origin of the word, one of which is grounded in Louisiana.

Daniel Decatur Emmett wrote "Dixie" for Bryant's Minstrels in 1859. *Wikimedia Commons.*

One of these legendary theories pertains to the term "Mason and Dixon." According to David Wilton, author of the book *Word Myths: Debunking Linguistic Urban Legends*, "Somewhere in the transition from meaning the boundary to denoting the Southern states, Mason was lost, and all that remained was *Dixie*." Wilton goes on to explain that the phrase "Dixie Land" became part of the vernacular as the result of its use in several songs performed by minstrel singer Daniel D. Emmett in 1859. The song titled "Dixie" became the unofficial national anthem of the Confederacy.

A less well-known theory concerns a Manhattan slave owner named Johan Dixy. He became renowned for his humane treatment of his slaves. It is said that slaves who were sold often spoke with fondness of their time in "Dixie's land" in New York. Wilton believes that this explanation is one of the most apocryphal.

An explanation that has its roots in New Orleans dates to the years just before the Civil War. A plaque posted outside of Walgreens at 134 Royal Street proclaims that the word *Dixie* originated at the Citizens State Bank, which once stood at this spot. During this time, the bank issued its own ten-dollar notes. These bills became known as Dixies because the French word for "ten," *Dix*, appeared on the side that was written in French. The other side of the notes was written in English. Because these notes were circulated primarily in the South, it stands to reason—for many residents of Louisiana—that this part of the country would then become known as Dixieland.

THE LOST CONFEDERATE SUBMARINE BASE

Shreveport

One of the most tantalizing mysteries of the Civil War concerns the location of a Confederate submarine base, as well as information collected by Union spies indicating that five submarines were built in Shreveport. One of the submarines was transported to Texas but was apparently lost in transit. The submarines were part of a plan to lay mines in the Red River to prevent a Union attack that never materialized. The existence of the submarine base was verified by historians Erick Brock and Katherine Brash Jeter, whose research uncovered documents indicating that the engineers and machinists who had worked on the *Hunley* were in Shreveport in 1865.

The fate of the four submarines has been the subject of speculation among historians and divers for years. In 2006, diver Ralph Wilbanks, who led the expedition that discovered the *Hunley* in 1995, conducted his second survey of the waterways around Shreveport in search of the submarines. The survey was underwritten by author Clive Cussler and his nonprofit, National Underwater and Marine Agency. After dragging side-scan sonars and magnetometers in lanes on mapped grides on the Red River, Cross Bayou and Cross Lake, Wilbanks found an old dock, old trucks from the 1920s and the remnants of the *Iron Duke*, a Civil War gunboat, but no submarines. He concluded that the submarines were abandoned and salvaged, probably melted down for steel.

Marty Loschen, director of the Spring Street Museum in Shreveport, disagrees, because Willbanks and his divers did not go as far as the shallower waters of Cross Bayou. Loschen believes that the submarines were just beyond the place that Willbanks ended his search. In 2014, Loschen and his brother were walking along a bank on Bowman's chute near Bowman and Dowling Streets, when they found rusted machinery and other artifacts. The fact that some of the trees had grown around the ironworks indicated that they had been lying on the bank for many years. Some of the trees were strangely formed, suggesting that they had grown around a curved object that had long since rotted away. Among the pieces of iron were metal straps, which Loschen believed had been used as stiffening ribs on submarines. This area is a half mile west of where the Confederate shipyard was located. Loschen theorized that the clandestine submarine base was located on an island around Cross Bayou.

As fascinating—and convincing—as Loschen's evidence might be, not all authorities agree with his findings. Gary Joiner, history professor at Louisiana University and expert on Confederate submarines, claims that the metal strips Loschen retrieved from Bowman's Inlet were not used in the tube-shaped submarines described in reports submitted by federal and Confederate spies. Joiner believes that the submarines are probably perfectly preserved in the sandy mud of the Cross Bayou.

THE CONFEDERATE GRAVE THAT BECAME A PARK

Marthaville

The Red River Campaign began in 1864, when Union general Nathaniel Banks's army of forty-five thousand troops advanced toward Shreveport in an attempt to crush the Confederate forces in western Louisiana. From there, Banks planned on moving on to Texas. Confederate general Richard "Dick" Taylor's army of eighteen thousand men conducted a series of hit-and-run attacks on the much larger Union army. On April 2, 1864, a contingent of Southern cavalry attacked the Yankees near Crump's Corner. Afterward, a young Confederate soldier showed up at the homestead of William Hodge Barnhill in search of water. All at once, three Yankee cavalrymen rode into the farm and shot the young soldier. He was buried by William Barnhill and his sons at the family farm.

Descendants of William Barnhill cared for the grave of the unknown Confederate soldier for ninety-eight years, until the State of Louisiana converted the farm into Rebel State Park. The centerpiece of the park is the Grave of the Unknown Confederate Soldier. The Louisiana Country Music Hall of Fame is also located in the park. On Memorial Day 2011, a Confederate grave dedication service was conducted for the unknown soldier by the Sons of Confederate Veterans and United Daughters of the Confederacy.

THE ST. FRANCISVILLE CIVIL WAR TRUCE

St. Francisville

Unofficial truces during the Civil War were fairly common. Occasionally, Union and Confederate soldiers would declare a "soldier's truce" when they needed to share food; trade for coffee, whiskey or tobacco; and share war stories. Noted military historian Ed Bearss said that their commanding officers disapproved of these truces for fear that their soldiers might inadvertently impart sensitive information to the enemy. Most of these truces have been lost to history. However, the truce that was held on the weekend of June 13–15, 1863, is forever etched in the collective memory of the residents of St. Francisville.

In October 1862, Lieutenant Commander John E. Hart was placed in command of the *Albatross*, replacing the captain when he was relieved of duty. In the spring of 1863, *Albatross* was one of Admiral David Farragut's fleet of seven ships that had been dispatched to destroy Confederate placements on the bluffs overlooking the Mississippi. On May 4, 1863, the *Albatross* and two other ships saw action on the Red River, doing battle with two Confederate steamers. In June 1863, the *Albatross* narrowly avoided being hit by the Confederate cannons on the bluffs at Port Hudson. While Hart was stationed above Port Hudson, he wrote a cheerful letter to his wife. Four days later, he killed himself. Naval records indicated he "suicided" while in the throes of delirium brought on by yellow fever. However, the surgeon, Dr. William Burge, said Hart had been suffering from depression for several months. In his suicide note, Hart wrote, "I am a dyspeptic. Will God forgive this rash act? It has been a mania with me for years. God knows my suffering."

The officers on board the *Albatross*, who were Masons like Hart, did not want his remains consigned to the river. On June 12, a party was sent to St. Francisville in a boat under a flag of truce to see if there were any Masons in town. The White brothers, who were living near the shore, told the group that there was indeed a Masonic lodge in town and that its senior warden, W.W. Leake, could be found among the Confederate forces in the area. The request for a Masonic funeral was forwarded to Leake, who honored the request. Leake believed it was his duty to bury Hart as a fellow Mason, even though he was a Yankee. The surgeon and Hart's fellow officers brought his body up from the river. They were met by W.W. Leake and a few other

Built in 1860, Grace Episcopal Church was the site of the St. Francisville Civil War truce in 1863. *Wikimedia Commons.*

Masons. The procession included a squad of marines at trail arms. It ended at Grace Episcopal Church. Hart was interred at the Masonic burial plot at Grace Episcopal Church. Many people believe that the *Albatross* had used Grace Episcopal Church for target practice just prior to his death. However, according to Christopher Pena, who received a grant from the state of Louisiana to research Hart's death and funeral, the ship's log mentions no such incident. St. Francisville was shelled on January 1864, almost one year later. The actual date of the funeral has been a point of contention, as well. Although the ship's log gives the date of the funeral as June 12, church records list it as June 13.

Since 1999, St. Francisville has staged a reenactment of John Elliot Hart's funeral, called the Day the War Stopped. Over the years, the reenactment has featured a number of different programs, including a Civil War encampment. The role of William Walter Leake has been played by a number of different men, including Leake's great-great-grandson. Several of Hart's and Leake's descendants have attended the ceremony, as well.

2.
LEGENDARY CEMETERIES

St. Louis Cemetery No. 1

New Orleans

St. Louis cemetery No. 1 is the second-oldest cemetery in New Orleans. The first cemetery exists under the paved streets of the city. St. Louis Cemetery No. 1 was founded in 1789 in a swampy plot of land outside of the city to prevent contagion from spreading to the general populace. Originally, the cemetery was twice as large as it is now. By 1815, it was reduced to one block, bordered by Basin, Treme and Conte Streets. The cemetery, with its above-ground tombs, was modeled on the Pere Lachaise Cemetery in Paris, except for the fact that the bodies were buried under the tombs in the Paris cemetery. New Orleans's Spanish colonial government might have followed the example of Barcelona's Poble Nou cemetery, where the bodies are slid inside the tombs. In St. Louis Cemetery, the above-ground burials were essential because of the city's high water table. In some of the older tombs, two or three coffins might have been stacked on top of each other. The original cemetery plots were laid out haphazardly, creating a maze-like pattern. Years later, the plots were arranged in Catholic, non-Catholic, Protestant and "Negroes" sections. The most famous burials in St. Louis Cemetery include the tombs of William Claiborne (1775–1817), the first American governor of Louisiana; Home Plessy (1862–1926), the subject of the *Plessy v. Ferguson* U.S. Supreme Court case; Paul Morphy, world champion of chess; the pyramid-shaped tomb of Nicholas Cage, which, at the time of this writing, is still unoccupied; and of course, the tomb of Voodoo Queen Marie Laveau (1801–1881).

More than twenty thousand tourists visit St. Louis Cemetery No. 1 annually, and it is a safe bet that most of them go there to visit the tomb of Marie Laveau. She was buried in the tomb of her in-laws, the Glampon family. Although some scholars believe she might be buried somewhere else, the fact that this tomb is mentioned in her obituary makes it her most likely resting place. Her tomb is also listed in the burial records for St. Louis Cemeteries numbers 1 and 2. For many years, some visitors to her tomb have scrawled three Xs on the tomb's exterior. Others have left offerings, hoping that their wishes will be granted. Many people believed that the proper way to seek the Voodoo Queen's blessing was to scratch the Xs with a piece of brick from another tomb. Marking the tomb with Xs is no longer permitted because the practice has no basis in voodoo tradition. To prevent additional vandalism to the historic tomb, the city has limited visitation to the tomb to groups led by licensed tour guides.

Wrong Way Cemetery

Rayne

For centuries, people in the United States have been buried with their feet to the east and their heads to the west. Long before Christianity, pagans were buried this way because the sun rises in the east. Christians adopted this custom because the Star of Bethlehem comes in the east. In addition, Matthew 24:27 states, "For as the lightning comes from the east and flashes to the west, so also will the coming of the Son of Man be." The truth, however, is that not all graves face true east because magnetic compasses were not always used when graves were dug. Instead, gravediggers went by the position of the sun at sunrise, which changed every day of the year. Consequently, the direction was set by perception in many cases. In cemeteries where one or two graves faced west–east instead of east–west, the stories arose that the people buried there had committed a terrible sin, such as suicide.

In Rayne, Louisiana, one can find the only cemetery in the United States where all of the graves face north–south instead of east–west. No one knows for certain why the above-ground tombs at the Saint Joseph Catholic Church cemetery are buried this way. Many locals blame the north–south orientation on a mistake made by the gravedigger. In 1880, the entire town of Pouppeville, as it was known back then, was moved five miles to the north. The town fathers hoped that the town's fortunes would improve immensely if it was located closer to the main line of the Louisiana Western Railroad. In an effort to remake Pouppeville as a railroad town, the city council built a railroad station and renamed the town Rayne after a railroad employee. The cemetery was moved north along with the rest of the town. By the time someone pointed out that the graves were facing north–south instead of east–west, it was too late. In recent years, Rayne has embraced its unique cemetery by placing the Ripley's Believe It or Not article that mentions it in the lobby of the chamber of commerce.

LEGENDARY MINDEN CEMETERY

Minden

Located in northwestern Louisiana, Minden Cemetery is not far from Minden's downtown district. It was originally a private cemetery owned by Colonel and Mrs. S. John Landon Lewis. The oldest interment is the grave of Mary A. Smith, who died on April 22, 1840. Like many of the older grave markers in the cemetery, Mary A. Smith's was destroyed by a tornado on May 1, 1933. A few tombstones dating to 1843 are still standing, including the marker on Sarah Emily Pennell's grave. The cemetery was deeded to the city of Minden in 1854. In 1864, twenty-two Confederate soldiers who died at the Battle of Mansfield (also known as Battle of Sabine Crossroads) were interred in unmarked graves in Minden Cemetery. An obelisk was placed at the site in 1936. Individual markers were not placed on the graves until 2008. All of the gravestones are marked with the inscription "Unknown Soldier," except for the headstone of Thomas L. Anderson, Private Colonel I, Thirty-First Texas Cavalry, born 1828, died 1864. His body was shipped home to his family.

Like many old cemeteries in the South, Minden Cemetery has acquired a haunted reputation. One of the tales concerns the Confederate graves. Locals said that every April 8, one could hear the spectral voices of the dead soldiers coming from the graves. In the early 1900s, a Confederate veteran

The oldest graves in Minden City Cemetery date to 1843, seven years after the founding of the city in 1836. *Wikimedia Commons.*

This obelisk identifies the unmarked graves of twenty-one Confederate soldiers killed at the Battle of Mansfield in 1864. *Wikimedia Commons.*

who visited the cemetery swore that he heard Thomas L. Anderson's voice calling roll. Interestingly enough, reports of the ghostly voices ceased after the Daughters of the Confederacy erected a gravestone on March 25, 2008. Some people familiar with the history of the Confederate section believe the spirits of the soldiers are at rest now that their graves are marked.

The other story people tell about Minden Cemetery concerns the "red tombstone." One of the darker tombstones is marked with red streaks that some say resemble blood. Legend claims that when one walks toward the tombstone, a cold breeze wafts by, and the red stains disappear. The tombstone's backstory involves the restless spirit of a young girl who committed suicide. Local skeptics believe that the tombstone's red color is actually the reflection of red light from the sign on the Coca-Cola Bottling Company of Minden or a flying red horse sign at a nearby petroleum bulk plant.

3

LEGENDARY LOCATIONS

OAK ALLEY

Vacherie

In 1830, a French Creole planter named Valcour Aime bought a large plot of land on the west bank of the Mississippi River for the purpose of growing sugar cane. In 1836, Aime's brother-in-law Jacques Roman acquired Bon Sejour plantation. Construction of the grand plantation house, which was supervised by Aime's father-in-law, commenced in 1837. The house was completed two years later. Following Roman's death from tuberculosis in 1848, his widow, Celine, assumed control of the plantation, but she proved to be a poor manager. To save Bon Sejour from bankruptcy, her son, Henri, took over. In 1866, a year after the Civil War, Henri's uncle Valcour Aimie sold the plantation at auction.

Over the years, the plantation passed into the hands of a succession of different owners. By the time Andrew and Josephine Steward purchased it in 1925, it had fallen into disrepair. Architect Richard Koch was hired to restore Oak Alley to its former splendor. Even sugar cane planting was reintroduced in the 1960s. At this time, it had acquired a new name—Oak Alley—after the double row of southern live oak trees that had been planted in the early 1700s. Josephine retained ownership of Oak Alley until her death in 1972, when it was bequeathed to the Oak Alley Foundation. Today, the Greek

Revival mansion is a bed-and-breakfast. Oak Alley owes its popularity not only to its twenty-eight stately oaks and its twenty-eight Doric columns but also to its signature legends.

One of Oak Alley's resident ghosts is usually identified as the spirit of Louise, the daughter of Jacques and Celine Roman. Just before the Civil War, Louise was courted by a number of different suitors. One day, she was standing in the front door awaiting the arrival of one of her beaux. As he rode through the alley of oaks, she could immediately tell that he had been drinking. Concerned about the possible threat to her good reputation, Louise returned inside and started running up the stairs. In her hurry to lock herself in her bedroom, Louise tripped on her crinoline petticoat and fell on the stairs. One of the hoops in her skit stuck her in the leg, causing her to bleed profusely. The servants and the local doctor tended to her wound and were able to stop the bleeding. However, within a few days, gangrene had set in, and the doctor was forced to amputate her leg. Fully aware that no one would want to marry her now, Louise entered a nunnery in St. Louis. A few years later, she founded her own convent in New Orleans. After she died, Louise was interred, along with her amputated leg, in a tomb at a small garden at Oak Alley. Her ghost is said to be the spirit of a young blond girl, whose spectral image was photographed sitting in a chair.

The ghost of Louise's mother, Celine, has also been sighted in and around Oak Alley. Dressed in a black or dark gray skirt, Celine's spirit rides on horse up the quarter-mile length of the alley of oak trees. She seems to enjoy walking on the balcony and the widow's walk. Many employees believe that she is awaiting her husband, Jacques, who walked back home from his private landing on the Mississippi River after returning by steamboat from his frequent business trips.

However, much of the paranormal activity at Oak Alley cannot be attributed to a single spirit. Rocking chairs have been known to rock by themselves. Objects left overnight on tables or desks have been moved to different locations. Tour guides have reported hearing spectral horses and the ghostly crying of a woman or a child. Objects have been known to fly across the room on their own. A ghostly carriage has been seen clattering up the roadway to Oak Alley. People have heard disembodied footsteps walking on the second floor. Strange noises emanate from the alley at times. Two of the tour guides, Helen Dumas and Alma Mitchell, were walking up the stairs inside the house one evening when they felt someone pinching them just below the knee. A tour guide, "Petesy" Dugas, was giving a tour of the old mansion one day, when suddenly, a candlestick flew across the room.

One of the scariest unexplained incidents took place when Oak Alley carpenters were attempting to repair the widow's walk. At the end of the day, they piled up the climbing harnesses they had been using inside the attic. The next morning, the men were shocked to find that all of their equipment was strewn across the attic floor. Security camera footage revealed that no one had entered the attic during the night. The fact that a paranormal investigation conducted in 2008 turned up no hard evidence has had little effect on the number of sightings consistently reported at Oak Alley.

OLD LOUISIANA STATE CAPITOL

Baton Rouge

After legislators decided to move the state capitol from New Orleans to Baton Rouge, construction of the new capitol commenced. Architect James H. Dakin's vision for the new building was a Neo-Gothic castle-like edifice on top of a bluff overlooking the Mississippi River. Not long after construction was completed in 1852, the capitol became embroiled in controversy. Some people lauded the its fairy tale–like ambience, including Sarah Morgan, author of *The Civil War Diary of a Southern Woman*. Others argued that it was a totally inappropriate emblem for a democratic seat of government. When Mark Twain viewed the capitol in 1862, he was outraged that "a white washed castle, with turrets and things…should have been built in this otherwise honorable place." After Admiral David Farragut's naval forces took New Orleans in 1862, the capitol was repurposed twice, first as a prison and then as a garrison for Black troops. The Union army abandoned the capitol after it was gutted—twice—by fires. When architect William A. Ferret completely rebuilt the capitol in 1882, he added some of his own touches, such as the spiral staircase and the stained-glass dome. In 1932, the old building was replaced by the new Louisiana State Capitol. For the next several decades, the old capitol housed the veterans' organization and the Works Progress Administration office. Following extensive renovations in the 1990s, the old state capitol became the home of the Museum of Political History. According to museum employees and visitors, the historic structure is home to a few ghosts, as well.

The old state capitol's most famous ghost is the spirt of Congressman Pierre Couvillon, who, in 1852, suffered a fatal heart attack in the senate

Built between 1847 and 1852 on a bluff overlooking the Mississippi River, the Old Louisiana State Capitol is now a museum. *wwltv.com.*

chamber during a fierce debate over gambling. Even though all signs point to the probability that Couvillon died elsewhere, his presence has been felt inside the old capitol for many years. His spirit is said to walk the halls of the old capitol at night. A security guard was making the rounds one night when he accidentally bumped into an invisible passerby. On a different night, a female security guard responding to a series of detector alarms going off in different parts of the capitol was surprised to find that the covers on the bed of the governor's room were rumpled, as if someone had been sleeping on top of them.

The second historical figure whose ghost makes an occasional appearance inside the Old State Capitol is that of Huey Long, who was shot inside the capitol on September 8, 1935, by a physician named Carl Weiss. Long died in a medical facility thirty-one hours later. Some people claim to have been followed by Long's ghost throughout the old building. It is said that the smell of cigar smoke inside the castle is a sign that Long's spirit is close by.

A female ghost has been sighted inside the capitol and on the grounds. This is probably the spirit of Sarah Morgan, whose parents donated the family land for use as the site of the state capitol. Her ghostly figure has also been sighted peeking out of the windows. Her love for the old castle goes back to her childhood, when she watched the capitol being built. Fittingly, Sarah Morgan is featured in the exhibit Ghost of the Castle, in which she recounts the history of the Old State Capitol.

Poltergeist activity attributed to no specific spirits abounds in the basement, which served as a hospital and a field hospital during the Civil War. Security guards have heard the grating sound of heavy doors opening and closing on their own. People walking down the empty hallways at night have the uneasy feeling that they are being watched by unseen eyes. Maintenance supervisor Carl Smith has had a number of paranormal experiences in the basement since he began working in the old capitol in 2008. One night, he was walking out of one of the stalls in the basement bathroom, when all at once, the door flew off its hinges, striking him in the back. Unsurprisingly, the paranormal groups that have investigated the old capitol at night have collected a large body of compelling evidence in the basement, including orbs, electronic voice phenomena (EVPs) and even the holy grail of ghost hunters—full-bodied apparitions. Some of the spirits have "gotten physical" with their overnight visitors, as well. The violent nature of some of these encounters suggests that the restless spirits of soldiers who were incarcerated there are taking out their anger on anyone unfortunate enough to cross paths with them.

THE OLD GOTHIC JAIL

DeRidder

In 1913, the Stevens-Nelson architectural firm in New Orleans was hired to design a courthouse and jail on a tract of land donated by the Hudson River Lumber Company. The Falls City Construction company completed the buildings in 1915, at a cost of $168,000. The Beauregard Parish Jail is one the few penal institutions in the United States that was built in the Collegiate Gothic design. It was also the first jail in the United States with a window in every cell. The jail was also unique in that every bathroom had its own facilities. At the time, only a handful of residents of DeRidder had

The Beauregard Parish Jail is the only penal institution in the United States built in the Collegiate Gothic style. Two men who murdered a cab driver were hanged here on March 9, 1928. *needpix.com.*

running water. Nevertheless, amenities in the jail were far from luxurious. Prisoners slept on black steel bunks with only a blanket. Access to every cell was provided by a large spiral staircase. The jail was built to accommodate approximately fifty prisoners. They were transported for trial through a tunnel leading from the jail to the courthouse to avoid attracting attention from onlookers. The bottom floor of the jail housed the kitchen and the jailers' quarters.

The Beauregard Paris Jail was known far and wide as the Old Gothic Jail because of its unique design. However, the building acquired the less flattering name of the Hanging Jail because of a high-profile execution that took place there. On Mary 9, 1928, two prisoners, Joe Genna and Molten Brasseaux, were hanged in the jail for murdering a taxi driver, J.J. Brevelle, while he was driving them to a rural destination. A floor was built on top of the rail of the third-floor stairway, and the bodies fell through a trap door in the center. The hangman was Deputy Sheriff Gill. In the 1950s, the execution was immortalized in a song by Sam Pruitt called "The Hanging Jail."

The jail was closed in 1984. Today, it is open for tours on Monday through Friday at 10:00 a.m., 11:00 a.m., 1:30 p.m. and 3:00 p.m. Over the years, a number of tour guides have had strange experience inside the jail. The director of the jail, Lori Darbonne, has heard a number of disturbing noises. Cleo Martin, the administrative assistant for the Tourist Commission, attributes some of the old jail's eerie atmosphere to a strange stain on the wall of the basement tunnel. There's an image that comes up on the wall, usually in the morning time, that resembles the face of a demon. You can see a hood around its face and where two horns come out, and you can see the eyes, but when we check the same spot in the evening, it transforms into an angel. According to Gary Crowe, whose father was a jailer at the facility, another weird image was captured in a photograph taken inside the jail years ago by one of the employees: "They didn't know when they took the picture, but when it was developed, it looked like a man sitting on the front porch smoking a pipe."

Unsurprisingly, the jail is also popular with paranormal groups. Lori Darbonne was present during one of these investigations. She was listening to one of the EVPs recorded that night and posted on the group's website when she was filled with a sense of dread: "I clicked on the fourth soundbit and I heard the voice say, 'Do you know that you're dead?' I remembered that was the question they asked in there that had given me chills…and what I heard it say was 'I'm alive, I'm alive.' It scared me so bad that day I immediately clicked off of it, and I never told a soul. It scared me that bad."

The Beauregard Parish Jail has capitalized on the public's interest in the paranormal by offering Lantern Tours on select Friday and Saturday nights. In the first half of the tour, guides turn off the lights while they present the history of the jail and the ghost stories. Some of the tour guides share their own experiences in the jail. In the second half of the tour, participants are allowed to walk around the corridors and cells on their own. They are encouraged to collect evidence through still photographs, voice recorders and EVP detectors.

In 2018, the NOLA Ghost Hunters investigated the jail on a Gothic Jail Lantern Tour with the Beauregard Parish Tourist Commission. The cofounders of the group, David and Mark Laville, and their team of investigators set up seven infrared cameras throughout the jail. David was in the women's cell when he heard heavy footsteps. His brother Mark had a similar experience in the cell. Later on, the members were standing in the jailers' quarters when David felt a tugging at the back of his shirt. No one was standing behind him at the time. At 11:30 p.m., David was in one of the cells alone when, suddenly, he heard three loud banging sounds. Afterward, he learned that other members of the group had also heard the sounds.

SCHOOL SPIRITS OF THE ELLERBE ROAD SCHOOL

Southeast Caddo Parish

George Washington Carver School was opened as a segregated school for Black students in 1957. Because of the low population base in the school's service area, the student body was never very large. The school's numbers declined considerably after desegregation, resulting in its closure in 1973. The Baptist tabernacle moved its Baptist Christian College to the former school in 1981, but the college moved out four years later. The building has been abandoned since 1985. The Caddo Parish School Board, which still owns the old school, began leasing the site for livestock grazing in 1996.

The school probably would have slipped into obscurity if not for the legends that keep its memory alive. The best-known legend concerns a janitor who took advantage of a number of students; most of them kept quiet out of fear. One day, the janitor disappeared, along with some of the students he had molested. Afterward, the administration tried to return the school to a state of normalcy, but a horrendous fire that took the lives of several students forced the school to close its doors. Teenagers who venture out to the abandoned property at night believe that if they climb the rusty steps of the school's water tower, they will see their reflection on the day they die. It is also said that not long ago, a satanic priest and priestess performed unholy rituals near the water tower. Some locals believe that the ghosts that haunt the old school are the spirits of soldiers who died in a Civil War battle that was fought on the grounds. Young people eager to prove their courage by exploring the crumbling old school report seeing shadowy figures in the windows. Some people claim to have heard the voices of students in the hallways, as well as the maniacal laughter of the perverted janitor.

None of the stories people tell about the infamous school appear to be grounded in fact. A former student at George Washington Carver School and local historian Cheryl White of Louisiana State University Shreveport told a reporter for television station KTBS that the tales about the psychotic janitor and the devastating fire are apocryphal. However, recent evidence suggests that satanic rites might have been practiced at the site. Dr. White showed the reporter a photograph of the carcass of a wild boar that was slaughtered in front of the school, either by Satanists or by teenagers bent on perpetuating the legend of devil worshipers at the site. Dr. White does believe that the pentagrams and inverted pentagrams painted on the interior and exterior walls of the building reflect the presence of wiccans, pagans or Satanists.

The absence of verifiable facts has not prevented teens and adults from visiting the abandoned school—neither has the threat of arrest by local police, who are under orders to apprehend trespassers. The human need to explain the unexplained exerts a strong pull on people, resulting in the creation of legends in some cases and injury and death in others.

Devilish Doings at Frenchtown Road

Baton Rouge

Frenchtown Road Conversation Area near Biloxi is BREC's largest conservation area. The park, which opened in October 2013, lies at the confluence of the Comite and Amite Rivers. The park's trails stretch over three miles through 495 acres of Bottomland Hardwood Forest and Spruce Pine Hardwood-Flatwood Forest. The park is home to a variety of flora and fauna, as well as countless flocks of migratory birds. Several species of fish abound in the waterways, including the Amite River. Park rangers warn visitors to be on the alert for snakes, especially under wet conditions. According to the teenagers who flock to this area on the weekends, devil worshipers who practice their unholy rites on Frenchtown Road also pose a threat to interlopers.

Most of the infernal activity is said to take place near the narrow railroad trestle. The rumors of satanic activity at the old bridge peaked in the 1980s. Locals say that years ago "Welcome to the Gates of Hell" was spray-painted on one side of the bridge. Foreboding graffiti, like "go back now," was painted over years ago. Some people claim to have seen dead cats and chickens hanging from the ridge. Stones in the shape of a pentagram were found under the bridge. People said that the Satanists who gathered at the bridge at night would kidnap anyone foolhardy enough to interrupt their rituals. Dark figures carrying black crosses and satanic bibles have been sighted near the bridge. Chanting echoes through the woods on dark nights; cult members are said to have lived in an old house in the middle of a field near the bridge. Supposedly, a witch lived in the area, as well. It was, according to the teens who congregate at the bridge, "the last house on the left." A flashing red light has been seen in one of the windows of her house.

A number of other legends have been circulating around the bridge. One story that is told concerns a young man who took his date to the bridge and turned off the car's engine to scare her. When the engine would not turn on, the young man was visibly frightened. In a familiar variant of this tale, a maniac approached a stalled car and buried an axe in the hood of the car. It is also said that a group of young people standing in a field reported that the lights in their parked car turned on by themselves. The lights of a ghost train are also said to appear on the old bridge occasionally. Its shrill, lonely whistle has been heard many times around the bridge. Deaths that people say occurred at the bridge involve a man who was murdered and dismembered in the woods and a little girl who was hit by a train on the bridge. Her screams can be heard whenever a train crosses the bridge. The ghost of a man who hanged himself from the bridge wanders around the pilings.

Like most urban legends, the legends of Frenchtown Road have little or no basis in fact. The people who pass them down usually preface their narratives by saying something like, "This story was told to me by a friend of a friend who actually saw this happen." One can be sure that this particular oral tradition will continue to grow as long as the local teenagers continue to drive out to Frenchtown Road to party and, perhaps, have an encounter with the unknown.

THE HOTEL BENTLEY

Alexandria

Legend has it that Joseph Bentley decided to build a new hotel after being refused a room at the Ice House Hotel. He hired architect George R. Man to design a hotel similar to the Capitol Hotel in Little Rock, Arkansas. Construction of the hotel was completed in 1907, but it did not open its doors to the general public until August 10, 1908. An eight-story wing, complete with eighty rooms, was added in 1933. Bentley lived in a lavish apartment with a private elevator on one of the top floors. A number of celebrities, like Roy Rogers and John Wayne, spent the night at the Hotel Bentley. During World War II when the U.S. military used Alexandria as a training site, the Bentley served as quarters for several of the commanders, including Dwight Eisenhower, George S. Patton and Omar Bradley. The hotel prospered throughout the 1950s, but business began to drop off in the early 1960s. It closed toward the end of the decade and stood abandoned for almost ten years. The future of the Bentley Hotel began to look brighter after it was added to the National Register of Historic Places in 1979. The old hotel was saved by real estate developer Buddy Tudor, who bought it in the early 1980s. Over the next five years, Tudor spent millions of dollars repairing the dilapidated luxury hotel. The fully restored Bentley Hotel reopened in 1985. Tudor sold the hotel to a New Orleans investment group in the late 1990s. A few months later, the group sold it to Bob Dean, who finally shut it down in 2004. On October 11, 2012, an investment group headed by local entrepreneur Jenkins purchased the hotel from Bob Dean. Jenkins initiated a multimillion-dollar restoration project involving the conversion of the seven-story tower into private residential units. Today, the ninety-three-room hotel stands as a living memorial to the grand hotels of years gone by.

A number of different spirits are said to have taken up residence inside the Hotel Bentley. Joseph Bentley's spirit has been sighted many times on the fifth floor and in his suite of rooms. The waitstaff in the Mirror Room Lounge claim to have seen him, as well. The unquiet spirit of a little girl who

A timber baron, Joseph Bentley, constructed the Hotel Bentley in 1907. It was added to the National Register of Historic Places on November 15, 1979. *Wikimedia Commons.*

plummeted down an elevator shaft occasionally makes an appearance inside the hotel. A male ghost has been sighted peering over the railings of the grand staircase, which he fell from in 1985. Lured to the Hotel Bentley by the reports of paranormal activity, the crew from the *Ghost Hunters* television show conducted an investigation there in 2011. The evidence they collected included phantom footsteps and the faint sound of someone singing. The investigators also elicited thumping sounds on command. Apparently, some of the occupants of the hotel never want to leave.

LEGENDARY LOYD HALL PLANTATION

Cheneyville

Loyd Hall is one of the most legendary plantations in Louisiana. This two-and-a-half-story brick house overlooking Bayou Boeuf was built by William Loyd in 1820. The story goes that William was the black sheep of the Lloyd family in England, which was connected to the Lloyds of London insurance company. After arriving in the United States, William decided to separate himself from his distinguished family by dropping the second *l* in his last name. He purchased six hundred acres of land to grow indigo, corn, tobacco and sugarcane. He worked the land with sixty-nine slaves. Loyd envisioned building a plantation house that would be the showplace of the Bayou Boeuf region. However, Loyd's neighbor, Civil War governor James Madison Wells, was not impressed. He referred to the beautiful mansion with the double porch and white columns with iron lace trim as "Loyd's Folly." Despite his wealth, Loyd soon acquired a negative reputation. The damage inflicted on the kitchen doors by American Indians indicates that his relationship with the local tribes was far from congenial. During the Civil War, Loyd served as a double spy for both the Union and the Confederate States of America. In 1864, Loyd was tarred and feathered and hanged from an oak tree in front of the plantation house.

Loyd Hall was occupied by a variety of owners in the twentieth century. In 1934, Mary Raxdale bought Loyd Hall. Renovation of the historic home was supervised by her brother, John Clarence Raxsdale Sr. Mrs. Virginia Fitzgerald restored the house again when her family purchased it in 1946. She lovingly preserved the original mahogany staircases, cypress woodwork and heart-pine flooring. Michael Jenkins acquired the property in 2007 and

Loyd Hall Plantation was built between 1816 and 1820 by William Loyd, the black sheep of the Lloyd London insurance dynasty. *pexels.com.*

opened it as a bed-and-breakfast. Loyd Hall was placed in the National Register of Historic Places in 1977.

Ghost stories abound at Lloyd Hall. One spirit is the ghost of a former slave on the plantation, a nanny named Sally Boston, who was apparently intentionally poisoned. Another female ghost is the spirit of a relative of William Lloyd, Inez Loyd, who leapt from the third-floor attic after being jilted by her fiancé at the altar. The third floor was also home to a school run by a young woman who lived in a room next to it. The story states that during the Civil War, she had an affair with a Union soldier who had deserted. After a few weeks, the soldier was shot and killed on the third floor, some say by the teacher's sister and others by an angry neighbor. The soldier's corpse was buried under the house to conceal the body. Sometime later, the owners moved the body to an undisclosed location somewhere on the grounds. Bloodstains on the third floor bear mute witness to the crime. Many people have seen the ghost of the unfortunate soldier playing his violin on the front porch.

Beulah Davis, who worked at the plantation for over forty years, said that many guests have had strange experiences at Loyd Hall. Some claim to have heard the sound of violin music being played on the front porch. Other people have said that items they placed in one spot before going to bed were moved to an entirely different location during the night. The aroma of coffee and food has been detected in different parts of the house, usually just before Sally Boston's ghost appears. Some locals claim that the ghosts are responsible for the fact that Loyd Hall has had a number of different owners. If this is indeed the reason, none of the owners are saying.

THE GIANTS OF CITY PARK

New Orleans

Live oaks are found in the coastal regions of the South, from Virginia to the Gulf Coast and into Mexico. These trees are called "live" oaks because their old leaves fall as the new leaves appear, giving them the appearance of being evergreen. Their massive limbs, which spread to the ground, are often twice the height of the tree. The world's biggest collection of these magnificent trees can be found in New Orleans's City Park. The largest can be found along the lagoon between Bayou Metairie and City Park Avenue. The oldest ones, like the McDonogh Oak and the Anseman Oak, are all that remain of an ancient forest that sprouted years before the earliest explorers scouted the area that was to become New Orleans. In the 1800s, local philanthropist John McDonogh donated the 100-acre tract known as the Allard Plantation to New Orleans for use as a city park. In 1891, the City Park Improvement Association, under the direction of a florist named Victor Anseman, initiated the development of the 1,300-acre park. More live oaks were planted in the park by the WPA in the 1930s and, in recent years, by citizen groups and the park administration. In 2005, Hurricane Katrina destroyed approximately two thousand trees in the park. The oldest and most legendary of these trees in the Old Grove survived the wrath of the storm.

The Dueling Oaks and the Suicide Oak acquired their names because of they were so far removed from the city. The 1938 WPA Guide to New Orleans states that the Dueling Oaks "served as a favorite spot at which affairs of honor were settled by sword or pistol in the days when satisfaction for an insult was obtained by spilling blood." Dueling was the preferred method of settling disputes for gentleman, until the practice was outlawed in the 1890s. One of these two trees was felled in 1949 by a hurricane. The remaining Dueling Oak is near the New Orleans Museum of Art. The

Affairs of honor were settled with pistols or swords under the Dueling Oaks in City Park until dueling was prohibited in the 1890s. *Wikimedia Commons.*

For many years, people in the depths of depression took their own lives under the Suicide Oak in City Park by shooting themselves or ingesting poison. *Wikimedia Commons.*

Suicide Oak, which stands on Victory Avenue near Marconi Drive, was the spot where people took their own lives in the Creole days of New Orleans. Most of these forlorn souls were bankrupts or spurned lovers who saw no other way out of their predicaments except by shooting themselves with pistols or ingesting poison. The huge tree with what appears to be a large gaping mouth became even more foreboding in appearance when it lost two limbs in the 1980s. One of the limbs still hangs lifelessly from the tree.

Today, the live oaks of New Orleans are one of the city's most popular destinations for tourists, many of whom have their pictures taken sitting on the lowest limbs of the trees or posing in a dueling stance in front of the Dueling Oak. The city celebrates its trees at Christmastime during its Celebration of the Oaks, when the LED Christmas lights draped over the limbs of trees attract hundreds of visitors to the park. The pride that New Orleans obviously takes in its mighty oaks ensures that they will be around for many years to come.

NOTTOWAY PLANTATION

White Castle

Born in Virginia in 1813, John Hampden Randolph moved to Mississippi with his family in 1820, when President James Monroe appointed his father as a federal judge. After marrying Emily Jane Liddell in 1837, Randolph devoted his time to raising cotton and the couple's eleven children. Convinced that he could make more money raising sugarcane, Randolph moved to Louisiana, where he bought a 1,650-acre cotton plantation. After converting the plantation to sugarcane, Randolph tripled his annual income within two years. In 1855, Randolph increased his landholdings with the purchase of 400 acres of highland and 620 acres of swam and Mississippi Riverfront land, where he planned to build a house worthy of his social standing. Randolph took great care to build a mansion that would rival the plantation home of his neighbor John Andrews. He hired renowned architect Henry Howard to design the house. It is constructed of cypress planks that had been cured in water for six years to make them impervious to termite damage. The bricks were made by hand on site. Slaves also crafted Nottoway's signature bousillage molding from horsehair, Spanish moss and river mud. Randolph's magnificent house with twenty-two white columns

Built by John Hampden Randolph in 1859, Nottoway Plantation is the largest antebellum plantation house in the South. *Wikimedia Commons.*

was completed in 1859, along with slave quarters, a schoolhouse, stables, wood cisterns and a greenhouse. He named his plantation home Nottoway, after the county in Virginia where he was born,

After Louisiana seceded from the Union, Randolph took two hundred of his slaves to a plantation in Texas while his wife, Emily, remained at Nottoway with their youngest children in the hope that the Yankees would spare the house. Even though Nottoway was occupied by both Union and Confederate troops during the Civil War, the only damage the house suffered was a single grapeshot pellet in the far-left column. According to legend, a Union officer spared the house when he realized that he had stayed there a few years earlier. After the Civil War, Randolph returned with fifty-three of his former slaves. The fortunes of the Randolph family declined drastically because of the drop in the sugar market. By the time Randolph died on September 8, 1883, the plantation had been reduced to eight hundred acres.

Nottoway had a number of different owners following Randolph's death. His widow, Emily, sold it to Desire Pierre Landry and his father-in-law, Jean Baptiste Dugas. Landry's widow sold the property to a sugar planter, Alfonse Hanlon, who lost the plantation to foreclosure in 1913. The next owner, Dr. Whyte G. Owen, bought Nottoway for $1,000. Hanlon tried, unsuccessfully, to run the sugar operation on the plantation; eventually, he was forced to sell 1,103 acres of farmland but was able to retain ownership of the plantation house. After Hanlon's death in 1949, Nottoway was passed down to his son, Stanford, whose wife, Odessa, inherited it after Stanford's death in 1974. In 1980, she sold the house to Arlin K. Dease but was allowed to live there until she died in 2003. Dease restored Nottoway and opened it to the public. An Australian named Paul Ramsay bought Nottoway in 1985, with the intention of converting it into a resort destination. In 1980, Nottoway was listed in the National Register of Historic Places.

The forty-room Italianate-Greek Revival plantation house is now a popular tourist destination. It is not unusual for many of the guests to come away from Nottoway with stories of personal encounters with the paranormal. Molly Hennesy-Fiske, a reporter for the *Los Angeles Times*, was told by Jim Denis, the night security manager, that her room, 14, was haunted by an apparition that harasses women with long hair. In fact, several of these women were so terrified that they left the room in the middle of the night. One woman was taking a shower when, all at once, the light went off. As her eyes were trying to adjust to the sudden darkness, she felt one cold hand on her neck, while the other one caressed her hair. Another female guest was taking a shower in a claw-foot bathtub when something seemed to shove the tub against the wall.

Denis went on to say that room 14 was not the only haunted place in Nottoway plantation. The carriage house is apparently haunted by the ghost of a girl who died there in the 1860s. Unlike the scary ghost in room 14, she is a comparatively friendly spirit, whose image was captured by a security camera while she was floating around the front parking lot. Denis recalled another occasion when he was cleaning a room and heard noises coming from the next room. He described the noises as the sounds of furniture being moved. The clerk at the main desk told him that the guests in that particular room had already checked out.

UNIVERSITY OF LOUISIANA: HAUNTED HARRIS HALL

Lafayette

In 1900, construction of the Southwestern Louisiana Industrial Institute commenced on twenty-five acres of land donated by the Girard Family. The Industrial Institute opened its doors on September 18, 1901, with one hundred students and eight faculty members. The institute changed its name to the Southwestern Louisiana Institute of Liberal and Technical Learning in 1921 and the University of Southwestern Louisiana in 1960. Then in 1999, the university acquired its present name, the University of Louisiana at Lafayette. The oldest buildings on campus are Foster Hall (1902) and DeClouet Hall (1905). The most storied building on campus, however, is Harris Hall.

Built in 1939, Harris Hall is the only remaining all-female residence on campus. Located at 544 McKinley Street on the corner of Boucher and McKinley, the dormitory was named after Thomas H. Harris, the former state superintendent of education. A close friend of university president Lethar Frazar, Harris was instrumental in the physical expansion of the university through the acquisition of WPA funding. Although the dormitory has been remodeled to meet the needs of today's students, Harris Hall's structure has been essentially unchanged since it was first built, including the reception hall, the reading room and a "date parlor," where the residents were allowed to meet their boyfriends. Nestled on the edge of the university's lovely Rose Garden Residence Hall area, Harris Hall's genteel façade belies a tragic episode that has haunted students for decades.

The story goes that sometime in the 1960s, a student, known only as Lilly, was taking the elevator at 11:46 p.m., when its safety control malfunctioned. The elevator plummeted to the bottom of the shaft, killing the girl. According to residents, every night at 11:46 p.m., the elevator gradually creeps down from the third floor to the first. As it nears the bottom, passengers feel a violent shaking, followed by a loud *boom* that can only be heard from the inside. Some residents believe that Lilly's ghost shakes the elevator while it is dropping to mess with them. Everything returns to normal after the elevator reaches the first floor, until the next night at 11:46 p.m. However, some students walking by the elevator during the day have reported feeling someone tugging on their backpacks. Despite the terror students experience on the elevator, Lilly is generally believed to be a benign spirit.

Some residents believe that Lilly's ghost is also responsible for strange occurrences in the dorm rooms. One former resident who lived on the first floor of Harris Hall in 2001 and 2002 said that several afternoons when she was taking a nap, she felt the bed move. It seemed like some invisible presence had just sat down at the foot of the bed. Another resident said that when she stayed at Harris Hall during sorority rush in 1996, the footlocker of the closet opened by itself. A young woman who lived on the top floor of Harris Hall from 1997 until 1998 reported that every night at 2:00 a.m., she heard the sound of furniture being moved in the attic. On another occasion, she and a group of her friends were talking about Lilly, when suddenly, they felt a cool breeze waft across the room. None of the windows or doors were open. Some girls, while walking up the stairs to their rooms, have heard disembodied footsteps behind them. One day, Ginny Rosewood, a resident at Harris Hall, decided on a whim to ask Lilly to help her find her missing earbuds. "Within, like, twenty minutes, my roommate found her earbuds in her wallet, which she carries around with her, and her keys are always in there," Rosewood said. She believes that Lilly plays occasional pranks on students as a release from boredom.

Spanish Moon

Baton Rouge

The building that houses the Spanish Moon bar was originally constructed in 1910 as a firehouse. The building was used as a temporary morgue for victims of the Great Flood of 1927. For the next fifty years, the former firehouse served as a feed store and, later on, a thrift store. In the 1970s, the building became a bar and flophouse for homeless people, drug addicts and pimps, among others. When the seedy watering hole was transformed into a bar called the Cypress Hollow, its clientele became much more upscale. In 1997, the bar acquired new owners and a new name: the Spanish Moon. By the 2000s, the Spanish Moon had become more than just a bar, acting as a concert venue that hosted bands, themed nights and karaoke events. In 2017, owners, Shane Courrege and David Pittman sold the Spanish Moon to Nick Thomas, the former owner of the Republic New Orleans, for $365,000. On June 9, 2018, the Spanish Moon hosted the Spanish Moon Festival, featuring nine bands, food trucks and artists to kick off the bar's facelift, which began on June 12. At the time of this writing, the renovations are still in progress.

Over time, the Spanish Moon became known as much for its ghosts as for its alcoholic spirits. Staff and patrons frequently caught sight of a young man walking through the bar, usually late at night, wearing 1950s-era clothing. Some employees claimed to have heard people talking upstairs after the bar closed. Delivery workers reported feeling as if someone was watching them as they made their early-morning drop offs. Bartenders cleaning up after hours also recalled feeling as if someone was standing behind them. Some of them heard the clinking of glasses when they were the only ones in the bar. Some bartenders have even refused to close up alone. Patrons playing pool have witnessed pool balls rolling off the table by themselves. A few patrons and employees have reported feeling someone tapping them on the shoulder when no one else was around.

The building that houses the Spanish Moon bar first served as a firehouse when it was built in 1910. Over the years, it has also housed a feed store and a temporary morgue. *Wikimedia Commons.*

For years, the ghost of a man wearing a 1950s-era suit has been seen walking through the bar area of the Spanish moon at night. *Wikimedia Commons.*

Beau Vorhoff, host of the paranormal show *Haunted*, might have proved this ghostly figure's existence. In 2014, his team captured the image of a man looking down at them from an upstairs balcony.

A couple of tragic incidents that took place in and around the bar could be responsible for the paranormal activity. Around the turn of the twentieth century, a little girl was run over by a horse-drawn wagon in front of the building. In 2013, a man was accidentally electrocuted inside the Spanish Moon. The true identity of the ghost—or ghosts—haunting the Spanish Moon has yet to be determined.

T'FRERE'S BED-AND-BREAKFAST

Baton Rouge

The house that has come to be known as T'Frere's Bed-and-Breakfast was constructed by W. Comeaux in 1880 in the Acadian colonial architecture style as part of the Comeaux plantation. Built with Louisiana red Cypress on a seventy-two-acre-plot, T-Frerer's is a typical Cajun-style residence. The main house has two floors, with a dining room, a parlor, a gazebo, an enclosed glass porch and four bedrooms, the Mary, the Leah, the 1890 and the Lafayette. The two guest rooms in the rear of the house are in the garçonnière, the nineteenth-century version of a "man cave," where the young men of the house entertained friends.

Although several different families have lived in the house over the years, the owners who have left the deepest impression are W. Comeaux's niece Amelie Comeaux and her husband. Not long after moving in, she died after falling into a well in behind the house. Many people believe that Amelie committed suicide, following the death of her husband and child to yellow fever. However, Richard Young, the current proprietor of T-Frerer's, says that there is another popular theory regarding Amelie's strange death: "A lot of people think that she was having an affair with somebody of mixed race, and the locals had such a problem with that, that they pushed her in the well." Because the Catholic Church ruled Amelie's death a suicide, it did not allow her body to be buried in a Catholic cemetery.

Legend has it that T'Frere's is haunted because Amelie was buried under the house. People say that Amelie makes her presence known by opening and closing doors and turning lights off and on. Occasionally, she rattles pots and pans in the kitchen. Some people believed that she splattered wax on the piano while someone was playing hymns to show her anger at being kept out of sacred ground. The piano was eventually removed from the house because guests were awakened by the sound of it playing in the middle of the night. Many guests have reported being tucked into bed and then being awakened during the night by someone pulling on their toes. Amelie's anger also surfaces when someone is talking about her in the house. More than once, the burglar alarm has seemingly turned itself on when people mention her name.

Several employees have had strange encounters in T'Frere's. Alexandrea Flores, an employee at the bed-and-breakfast, noticed that sometimes when someone walks toward a door, the doorknob turns on its own, and the door opens when no one is on the other side. She added that one day, she was whistling inside the house when she was alone, and she heard someone whistle back. Several years ago, an exterminator had the only sighting of a full-body apparition in T'Frere's. He was working in the attic, when all at once, the spectral figure of a woman wearing a rose-colored dress appeared from behind the chimney. She seemed to beckon him to come to her by speaking two words in French: *Viens Voir* ("come see").

T'Frere's owners have not actively promoted their ghost, but guests have been encouraged to draw their own conclusions. In October 2015, a reporter for the *Daily Advertiser*, Megan Wyatt, was allowed to conduct an overnight investigation at T'Frere's with Katie Duro, Megan Bergeron, Holly Trahan and Megan's mother. At 11:30 p.m., the troop moved upstairs to Durro and Bergeron's guestroom. Their hopes for some sort of evidence of a ghostly presence were raised when the lights started blinking on and off at 12:12 a.m., and 1:22 a.m., Megan and her mother returned to their guestroom and went to bed at 1:58 a.m. At 7:36 a.m., Megan woke up, disappointed because no paranormal activity had awakened her during the night. However, when her mother awoke seven minutes later, she told Megan that she had heard childish laughter in the middle of the night. It sounded to her like little kids were playing nearby, even though no children were in the house at the time. No one else experienced anything out of the ordinary during the investigation.

SHREVEPORT MUNICIPAL MEMORIAL AUDITORIUM

Shreveport

The Shreveport Municipal Memorial Auditorium at 795 Elvis Presley Boulevard was constructed between 1926 and 1929 as a memorial to the men who served in World War I. The Art Deco building was designed by Samuel G. Wiener Sr. and Seymour Van Os of the firm Jones, Roessle, Olschner & Wiener. For years, the 3,200-seat auditorium has served as a venue for concerts, musicals and plays, boxing matches and other special events. During World War II, soldiers were billeted inside the auditorium. It was designated a National Historic Landmark because, from 1948 to 1960, the Louisiana Hayride was broadcast from its stage, giving national attention to such country and rockabilly stars as Hank Williams, Johnny Horton, George Jones, Slim Whitman, Johnny Cash and Elvis Presley. The auditorium was renovated between 1994 and 2000. During this time, ramps, air conditioning and elevators were installed.

Historical tours of the Shreveport Municipal Memorial Auditorium have been held since 2000. After a few years, ghost tours were added because the strange sounds and experiences people witnessed. According to tour guide Teresa Michaels, a door in the foyer opens and closes by itself. A visitor to the auditorium captured the door's strange behavior on camera. A disembodied face has been seen in one of the doors leading to the floor seats. EVPs captured inside the auditorium include clapping sounds and a voice that says, "I love Johnny Cash." A tour guide said that one evening,

The Art Deco building that houses the Shreveport Municipal Memorial Auditorium was constructed between 1926 and 1929 as a memorial to the servicemen who fought in World War I. *Wikimedia Commons.*

she was walking down the stairs, when she felt something grab her hand and place it on the banister. When she removed her hand from the banister, an unseen force picked her up and carried her to the bottom of the stairs. The spirit of a girl in a blue dress is the most commonly sighted apparition in the auditorium. Visitors usually catch sight of her running around out of the corner of their eye. The most unsettling paranormal activity in the auditorium is the sound of a woman moaning in the restroom. Legend has it that a woman gave birth in the bathroom during the Louisiana Hayride in the 1950s.

Another terrifying encounter took place when a worker was setting up for a sporting event inside the auditorium. While he was moving chairs around, he saw a man sitting in one section of the auditorium. A few minutes later, he saw the same man sitting in a different section. After an hour or so, the workman went out to his truck to retrieve a tool. There, standing outside of the auditorium, was the same strange figure. He walked up the man and asked him if he needed help. The young man replied, "I just came to see what time the fights start." With a beguiling smile on his face, he slowly faded away. When the workman shared his strange encounter with his coworkers, he was surprised to learn that, years before, a young boxer who had been scheduled to fight in a match was killed in a car wreck while driving to Shreveport.

Several paranormal groups have investigated the Shreveport Municipal Memorial Auditorium. Louisiana Spirits Paranormal Investigations recorded several striking EVPs. One of the members was pushed and scratched while walking through the basement. Everyday Paranormal recorded a clear voice saying, "We Saw the Light." Later, the door to the ballroom opened right after one investigator had shut it. When the band the team had brought in played rockabilly music in an attempt to stir up the spirits, another door closed. In 2013, the SyFy Channel program *Ghost Hunters* filmed an episode at the Shreveport Municipal Memorial Auditorium. During the investigation, the spectral voice of a man was recorded. The investigators suspected that it might be the ghost of one of the other performers who has not quite left the building.

The Calcasieu Parish Courthouse

Lake Charles

Calcasieu Parish was originally created in 1840 from the Parish of Saint Landry. On December 8, 1849, Marion was selected as the seat of justice. The first courthouse in Marion was nothing more than a small log cabin. In 1853, the seat of justice was relocated from Marion to the east bank of Lake Charles, on the recommendation of Sheriff Jacob Ryan, who moved the original log courthouse on an ox to Lake Charles, with the help of a slave and a friend, Samuel Adams Kirby. Within a year, the rough log cabin was replaced by a new wooden courthouse. In 1891, a colonial brick building was constructed at the cost of $20,000. In 1910, a devastating fire destroyed the brick courthouse, along with many other buildings, in downtown Lake Charles. On April 4, 1911, the decision was made by the police jury to erect a new courthouse on the site of previous one. Designed as a replica of the Villa Copra in Vicenza, the brick-and-terracotta courthouse was completed in 1912 at a cost of $200,000. Between 1993 and 1998, the interior and exterior of the 1912 courthouse were extensively restored to the building's 1910 appearance. Today, the courthouse is home to the offices of the clerk of court, the registrar of voters, the sheriff's civil division and several others. The courthouse is also home to the ghost of the only woman who was executed by Louisiana's electric chair.

Annie McQuiston was born in 1916. When she was six years old, her mother died, leaving her without a stable influence in her life. Growing up, she drifted into the life of prostitution, drug addiction and alcoholism. Her life achieved a degree of normalcy when she married a boxer named "Cowboy" Henry, whom she credited with saving her from self-destruction, despite the fact that he was also an enforcer for several criminal syndicates in the state. At this time, she was going by the name of Toni Jo Henry. She and her husband had not been married very long before he was arrested and incarcerated in Huntsville. Desperate to be united with her husband, Toni Jo and a friend decided to travel to Huntsville and arrange for Cowboy's release. When their plan failed, the duo began hitchhiking home. While they were walking along the highway, they were picked up by a Ford Coupe driven by Arthur Calloway. On the way back to Louisiana, the two shot and killed Calloway. They compounded their crime by stealing his car, money and clothes.

Built in 1912, the Calcasieu Parish Courthouse was the site of the only electric chair execution of a woman in Louisiana. *Wikimedia Commons.*

Toni Jo and her accomplice were eventually captured. Toni Jo was tried and found guilty of murder. On the day of her execution inside the courthouse, multiple generators were brought in just in case the electric chair failed. According to a local historian named Adley Cormier, Toni Jo's hair was cut short before she was strapped into the electric chair. "Witnesses recount that the lights went dim [when the switch was pulled], grew bright and went dim again," Cormier wrote. "Then they were overwhelmed by the smell of burnt hair and cheap perfume.'

Toni Jo's grisly end gave rise to a fairly high level of paranormal activity inside the courthouse. Any strange occurrence that mirrors what happened on the day of Toni Jo's execution, like the dimming of lights, is attributed to her. Some employees and visitors have reported detecting the smell of perfume and burning hair inside the courthouse. The sound of a woman's footsteps is sometimes heard on the path she took on the way to the electric chair. Toni Jo's ghost is also blamed for turning on the electrical system, unlocking doors and talking when night guards are all alone. The most haunted spot in the courthouse is the Calcasieu Parish

Clerk's office. People who work there consider it to be bad luck to mention Toni Jo's name during election season. "You can never be too cautious during election season," Cormier said, "especially when the place you're voting in could be haunted."

USS *KIDD*

Baton Rouge

The USS *Kidd*, a Fletcher-class destroyer, was named after Rear Admiral Isaac Campbell Kidd Sr., who was killed on the USS *Arizona* during the attack on Pearl Harbor on December 7, 1941. Admiral Kidd's widow, Mrs. Inez Kidd, christened the ship when it was launched on February 28, 1943. On its first voyage, the *Kidd* flew the Jolly Roger from the foremast as it moved across New York Harbor to the Brooklyn Naval Shipyards. Fittingly, the crew chose Captain Kidd as the mascot. Once the crew had obtained permission from Mrs. Kidd and from the navy, the *Kidd* became the only ship in the history of the U.S. Navy to sail under a pirate flag. In another break from tradition, a WAVE (Women Accepted for Volunteer Emergency Service) named Anne Randle was placed on the list of personnel, despite the belief that having women aboard a ship was bad luck.

The *Kidd* was commissioned into service on April 23, 1943. After covering the sea lanes near Argentia, Newfoundland, the *Kidd* escorted new carriers from Norfolk to Trinidad. It also provided escort for USS *Alabama* and *South Dakota* in August 1943. The *Kidd*'s other duties included rescuing downed pilots, patrolling for submarines and participating in shore bombardment. The *Kidd* was attacked by eight Japanese bombers while picking up the crew of a downed plane from the Essex. While rescuing the two pilots, the crew of the Kidd shot down three Japanese planes. The *Kidd* saw action at Tarawa in November 1943 and in the Marshall Islands in January 1944. It also participated in the occupation of Guam in July and August, earning distinction for rescuing thirty-five carrier personnel. The *Kidd* sailed to Pearl Harbor for repairs in August 1944 and to the Mare Island Naval Shipyard in California for a major overhaul.

In February 1945, the *Kidd* sailed back to the western Pacific, joining Task Force 58. On March 19, 1945, the *Kidd* guarded carrier USS *Franklin*, which had been severely damaged in a kamikaze attack. Then on Wednesday, April

The USS *Kidd*, a Fletcher-class destroyer, was severely damaged during a kamikaze attack on April 11, 1945. Thirty sailors died and fifty-five sailors were wounded. *Wikimedia Commons.*

11, 1945, the *Kidd* suffered its most serious damage during the entire war. A kamikaze pilot hit the boiler room, killing all of the sailors inside. The bomb the pilot had been carrying crashed through the entire ship, exiting through the other side, where it blew up. Thirty men were killed, and fifty-five were wounded. The *Kidd* limped away, protected by the covering fire from its sister ships. While heading toward Ulithi Atoll, the crew buried the dead at sea on April 12, the same day that President Franklin Delano Roosevelt died. After temporary repairs were made, the *Kidd* was en route to Japan a few days after the Enola Gay dropped the atomic bomb on Hiroshima. After returning to San Francisco, the *Kidd* was decommissioned on December 10, 1956.

The *Kidd* was commissioned back into service on March 28, 1959, during the Korean War. In July, it joined Carrier Task Force 77 at Wonsan, Korea. In September 1951, the *Kidd* was assigned to patrol the Formosa Strait. Following repairs in San Diego, the it returned to bombardment duty, rescuing downed pilots, as well. At the harbor in Wonsan, the *Kidd* destroyed several shore batteries. In March 1953, the destroyer departed Korea for San Diego. While sailing off Pierpoint Landing in Long Beach Harbor on April 21, 1953, the Swedish freighter *Hainan* struck the *Kidd*, leaving a fifteen-foot V-shaped hole reaching three feet below the waterline. Once again, damages were repaired, and the *Kidd* was in service on May 11, 1953.

Between 1954 and 1959, the *Kidd* participated in a series of WestPac Cruises throughout Asia and Australia. The *Kidd* joined naval forces during the Suez Crisis in 1956 and patrolled the straits between Formosa and China in 1958. In 1959, it was involved in the mobilization of military force in response to the construction of the Berlin Wall. Beginning on November 24, 1962, the *Kidd* served as a training ship for naval reservists.

The *Kidd* was decommissioned for the last time on June 19, 1964, with twelve battle stars to its credit. On May 23, 1982, the *Kidd* was towed from Philadelphia to Baton Rouge. Since then, it has been restored to its 1945 specifications and is the only remaining destroyer in its World War II appearance. Moored in the Mississippi River in Baton Rouge, the *Kidd* is a major component of the USS *Kidd* Veterans Museum. The ship is still serving its country, this time as a memorial to the brave service and sacrifices of its crew and of all the sailors in the U.S. Navy.

Like many World War II–era ships that experienced damage and death in battle, the USS *Kidd* is said to be haunted. For years, visitors have reported seeing the images of a single arm or leg on the deck. The severed limbs appear to be moving in agony. In the control room, one visitor took a photograph of a sailor wearing a cap leaning over the control panel. A man who was part of a group that was spending the night on the ship said that one of the children on board asked him if he had seen a ghost that was walking around and making sure that everyone was tucked in for the night. A woman who was walking through the sleeping quarters below deck reported feeling a heaviness in the air. Her discomfort was amplified by the sensation that someone was watching her. Another visitor took a photograph of one of the beds in the sleeping quarters. Under the bed was a blue orb. Her friend captured several yellow orbs hovering around the gift shop. The ghostly voices of sailors have been heard in the sleeping quarters, as well.

Because of the USS *Kidd*'s authentic appearance, it has been the subject of two motion pictures. In September 1958, the *Kidd* and the submarine USS *Redfish* were featured in the film *Run Silent, Run Deep*, with Clark Gable and Burt Lancaster. In 2018, the movie *Greyhound*, starring Tom Hanks, was filmed on the ship. With money received from the production company, the museum was able to purchase expensive technology, including a virtual reality prototype that enables visitors to shoot down kamikazes.

The Diamond Grill

Alexandria

Located on the Red River at 924 Third Street, the first incarnation of the Diamond Grill was a jewelry store built by a Scottish immigrant. River traffic accounted for most of the jewelry store's business. Several years later, Carl A. Schnack bought the business. Schnack's jewelry store soon gained a reputation for its high-quality merchandise. The Art Deco structure stood empty for a while after the jewelry store moved in the 1990s. The historic building's fortunes improved immensely when a local attorney and the grandson of the original builder purchased it with the intention of converting it into an upscale restaurant. They named it the Diamond Grill to recognize its history as a jewelry store. Today, the Diamond Grill is known for its delicious seafood, juicy steaks and ghostly presence.

According to legend, the Diamond Grill is haunted by the ghost of a woman named Stella. Staff and customers who have seen her apparition describe her as a well-dressed, attractive young woman. Supposedly, she is said to be a patron or a former employee of the jewelry store who is unhappy with its transformation into a restaurant. She expresses her displeasure by disrupting the daily routine inside the restaurant. She is also blamed for moving jewelry from one place to another in the restaurant. Glasses and bottles have been known to fly off the shelves in the mezzanine-level bar. A black amorphous shape has been sighted on the third floor. Doors lock and unlock on their own. Waiters have complained about being intentionally tripped by an invisible foot. On one occasion, all of the glasses in a storage closet were found broken to pieces.

In 2011, an episode of the SyFy television show *Ghost Hunters* was filmed in the Diamond Grill. During the night, the investigators caught the image of an apparition peeking around the door. They also witnessed a door opening on its own. The members recorded several startling EVPs. In a bar on the second floor, the group recorded a clear voice calling out the name of one of the ghost hunters. The members also heard the sound of something being dragged across the floor. After the investigation, the group concluded that an intelligent haunting was taking place that night at the Diamond Grill.

Houmas House

Burnside

In the 1700s, settlers began moving into the fertile lands formerly occupied by the Houmas Indians. In 1803, Donaldson and Scott built a new center hall cottage in front of a 1700s-era house built by the French. General Wade Hampton acquired the property in 1829, transforming the Donaldson House into a mansion fitting for a planter and his wife. When General Wade Hampton I died in 1835, the estate was passed down to his son Wade Hampton II. He, in turn, gave the plantation to his stepsisters, Caroline Hampton Preston and Susan Hampton, and his stepmother, Mary Cantey Hampton. Following the death of Susan Hampton, Mary Cantey Hampton gave her share of the plantation to Caroline Hampton Preston and her husband, John Smith Preston, who was a planter, politician, banker and soldier. By 1848, thirty family members, as well as a large number of servants, lived at

Known as the Sugar Palace, Houmas House was transformed in 1829 into a Greek Revival mansion fit for a wealthy sugarcane farmer and his family. *Marilyn Brown.*

Houmas House. On April 15, 1858, John Burnside purchased the plantation for $1 million. The plantation now included twelve thousand acres and over 550 slaves. That same year, Burnside sold his trading and dry goods store for $2 million, with the intention of becoming a sugar planter. He soon began buying other plantations along the Mississippi River, earning himself the title "Sugar Prince." In 1881, when he died at age seventy-one in White Sulphur Springs, West Virginia, he left the property to his boyhood friend Oliver Beirne, who asked his son-in-law, William Porcher Miles, to manage the estate. After Beirne died in 1888, his five grandchildren inherited the $5 million estate.

In 1892, Beirne's grandchildren transferred their interest to the Miles Planting Company and appointed their father, William Porcher Miles, president. Houmas House was enlarged in the 1890s, when it was connected to the French House in the rear. A library was installed on the first floor of the mansion. Following the death of William Porcher Miles, William P. Miles Jr. and his sisters inherited the plantation. Miles married Harriet Waters, age twenty-five, of New Orleans. She was twenty years younger than her husband. The couple turned Houmas plantation into a showplace, throwing lavish garden parties and hunting excursions. When a poor sugar crop forced the Miles family to sell off the plantation, they used Houmas House as a retreat for the weekends and holidays. Houmas House passed out of the hands of the Miles family when it was sold to Dr. George Crozat in 1940. He hired architect Douglass Freret to remodel the house in the Williamsburg federal style. The belvedere railings and cupola ornaments were removed, as well as several outbuildings. Dr. Crozat adorned the interior of the mansion with early Louisiana antiques.

After the estate of Dr. Crozat auctioned off all the furnishings of the mansion in the spring of 2003, it was sold at auction to a New Orleans businessman named Kevin Kelly. He immediately set about restoring the gardens and the mansion itself. Because Houmas House had been remodeled in a variety of styles over the years, he decided to choose the best features from each pattern. In November 2003, Kelly opened the plantation for tours, reserving the mansion as his private residence.

The spirits that haunt the Houmas House Plantation and Gardens were spawned by two tragic events. Prior to the 1930s, a great alley of live oaks lined the grand lawn from the River Road. One of the earliest owners of the house, John Burnside, was a bachelor who called the twenty-four majestic oaks the "Gentlemen." Following the Great Flood of 1927, the construction of higher levees became one of the major projects of the Works Progress

Houmas House is furnished with lavish nineteenth-century antiques. The centerpiece of the house is this magnificent three-story spiral staircase. *Marilyn Brown.*

Administration. Sixteen of the "Gentlemen" became victims of progress. They took their revenge, however, when sixteen men died as they were floating the trees down the river to the mills in New Orleans. Afterward, the eight remaining oak trees morphed into twisted caricatures of themselves. Some locals believe that the oaks became disfigured when they were occupied by the spirits of the drowned workers.

Three separate occurrences might have generated the second of the two ghosts that call Houmas House home. In 1848, Colonel John Preston's lively young daughter suddenly took ill. She and her family moved to Columbia, South Carolina, where she died. In 1990, another little girl—the seven-year-old daughter of Colonel William Porcher Miles and his wife, Harriet—died as well. She was buried in the family cemetery by the river. In the 1930s, the cemetery disappeared under the new levee. A number of graves were disturbed in the process. None of the tour guides or guests who have seen the ghost of the little girl in the blue dress know her identity. She is a shy little spirit who vanishes when people follow her. Her most famous manifestation took place in 2003, after Kelly had started renovating the historic house. One of the workmen saw a little girl between seven and ten years old, walking down the freestanding stairway. She seemed so real that the man was concerned for her welfare amid the construction. Later that evening, two other works saw a little girl in a blue dress with dark eyes and hair. She vanished before they could approach her. Some parapsychologists believe that spirits inside a house are "stirred up" when drastic changes are made to the property. Perhaps this is the case with the little ghost of Houmas House.

LAURA PLANTATION

Vacherie

In 1785, a group of Acadian immigrants settled on an area of high ground that had been the location of Tabiscanja, a large Colapissa village, earlier in the century. In 1755, Andre Neau obtained the plot of land on which Laura Plantation is now located from a French royal land grant. In 1804, President Thomas Jefferson granted a French naval veteran of the Revolutionary War, Guillaume Duparc, a stretch of land along the Mississippi, which included the Neau plantation. Between 1804 and 1805, Duparc built a U-shaped raised Creole plantation house with two back wings around a central courtyard. Unlike most Creole houses, which have Greek Revival woodwork, the interior of the big house at Laura Plantation has Federal-style woodwork. The detached kitchen was built in the back to prevent fires from spreading to the main house. Over the years, the Duparc family expanded the size of the sugar cane plantation to twelve thousand acres. One mile behind the house was the sugar mill. Just before the Civil War, 186 slaves occupied sixty-nine cabins along the road. A notable descendant of the slaves who lived and worked at Laura Plantation was Fats Domino, a popular American singer-songwriter from the 1950s. The Colapissa Indians lived behind the house until 1915.

In 1876, two members of the Duparc family divided up the property between themselves. In 1891, a descendant of the Duparc family sold the property to A. Florian Waguespack, on the condition that the plantation retained the name of Laura. The Waguespack family operated the plantation until 1884. The architecture of the main building is distinctive

Revolutionary War veteran Guillaume Duparc built this U-shaped raised Creole plantation house between 1804 and 1805 on land acquired through a French royal land grant. *Marilyn Brown.*

because of its Norman roof truss. Laura Plantation is also historically significant because it is one of only fifteen plantations in Louisiana with several outbuildings and two slave cabins. Laura Plantation is in the National Register of Historic Places and is included on the Louisiana African American Heritage Trail. Today, the plantation is an interpretation center for history and heritage tourism.

Laura Plantation is of particular interest to folklorists because of its connection to Alcée Fortier. Born on June 5, 1856, in St. James Parish not far from Laura Plantation, he was descended from sugarcane planters, merchants, military men and politicians. Fortier started out teaching French at the University of Louisiana and then became a professor of romance languages at Tulane University. By the end of his academic career, Fortier had become dean of Tulane Graduate School. Fortier visited Laura Plantation in the 1870s to collect stories from freedmen in the area. Most of these tales were brought to Louisiana by enslaved Senegalese from the Senegambia region of Africa in the 1720s. They related the stories in a Creole dialect based on French and African languages. Two of the most popular characters

In the 1870s, Alcee Fortier collected folktales from freedmen who lived in slave cabins like these on Laura Plantation. *Marilyn Brown.*

were Compair Lapin, a clever rabbit, and Compare Bouki, a strong, foolish hyena. Some of these stories were published in the *Journal of American Folklore* in the 1880s. Fortier published even more of these tales in two book-length collections, *Bits of Louisiana Folk-lore* (1888) and *Louisiana Folk-tales* (1895). In the 1990s, the historical and cultural significance of the tales Fortier had collected compelled preservationist Norman Marmillion to set up a for-profit company with the purpose of developing a ten-year plan for the restoration of Laura Plantation.

COURT OF TWO SISTERS

New Orleans

The Court of Two Sisters is a restaurant located at 613 Royal Street. The 600 block of Royal Street is known as Governor's Row because five governors lived there. The second French royal governor of Louisiana, Sieur Étienne de Périer, was the first resident at 613 Royal Street. Another French governor, the Marquis de Vaudreuil, also lived at 613 Royal Street later. The French townhouse that is now known as the Court of Two Sisters was built in 1832 for Jean Baptiste Zenon Cavelier, the president of the Bank of New Orleans. His family remained in the Cavelier until 1854. One of the subsequent owners, Emile Angaud, bought the house in 1886. Emile's daughter-in-law, Bertha, and her sister, Emma Camors, opened a notions shop in the building the same year. Their shop, called the Court, sold Mardi Gras costumes, formal gowns and perfume to upper-class women in New Orleans. The sisters' favorite customers were treated to tea and cake in the adjacent courtyard. Following the death of Bertha's son in 1904, her sister's children inherited the property. Bertha and Emma were forced to close their shop not long thereafter, when the influx of Italian immigrants replaced the Creoles who had supported their business. The sisters, who were only two years apart in age, were so close that they remained together for the rest of their lives. Both of them died in the winter of 1944, only two months apart. They are buried side by side in St. Louise Cemetery Number 3.

The Court of Two Sisters was named after the daughters of Emile Angaud, who operated a notions shop here between 1886 and 1904. *Alan Brown.*

Between 1925 and 1934, the building that housed the sisters' shop became a bistro, a refreshment stand and a speakeasy. During and shortly after World War II, the restaurant, under Jimmy Cooper, catered to the tourists and service men and women who flocked to New Orleans. In 1963, the restaurant passed into the hands of Joe Fein Jr., who set about restoring it. His sons and grandchildren took over the day-to-day operation of the Court of Two Sisters, which is renowned in New Orleans for its Jazz Brunch and its gourmet Creole dishes.

The Court of Two Sisters is also known for its legends, the earliest of which focuses on the "Charm Gates" at the entrance, which were supposedly blessed by Queen Isabella of Spain. According to legend, their "charm" is passed over to anyone who touches the gates. People also say that, pirate Jean Lafitte killed three men in three separate duels in the courtyard under the willow tree when he was twenty years old. The wishing well in the courtyard is called the Devil's Wishing Well in honor of Marie Leveau, the Voodoo Queen of New Orleans. The ghosts of the two sisters, Bertha and Emma, have been sighted walking around their former notions shop. They are often seen sitting at a table in a corner of the courtyard. None of the waitstaff or customers feel threatened by their presence. Bertha and Emma seem to be watchful spirits who will always have a connection to 613 Royal Street.

THE BEAUREGARD KEYES HOUSE

New Orleans

The site of the Beauregard-Keys was originally owned by the Ursuline nuns, who sold the plot of land in 1825. Joseph Le Carpentier constructed the house at 113 Chartres Street in 1827. It was designed by Francois Correjolles, who combined the elements of a Creole cottage with Greek Revival features. Carpentier was the grandfather of Paul Charles Morphy, a world-famous chess master, who was born in the house. In 1833, John A. Merle, the consul of Switzerland, bought the house. Later, an adjoining garden was added. Dominique Lanata, a local grocer, bought the house in 1865 with the intention of renting it out. Pierre Gustave Toutant Beauregard and his second wife, Caroline Deslonde, became Lanata's first tenants. Beauregard and his wife had a brief honeymoon in the house, until he rode off to war.

Right: After the Civil War, Confederate general Pierre Gustave Toutant Beauregard lived in the Beauregard-Keyes House between 1866 and 1868. *Wikimedia Commons.*

Below: According to legend, Corrado Giacana and his family killed three Mafioso gunmen and wounded one during a dinner party in the early 1900s at the Beauregard-Keyes House. *Alan Brown.*

After the Civil War, Beauregard lived in the house from 1866 to 1868, when he moved to a different house at 934 Royal Street.

In 1908, the wealthy Giacona family bought the house at 113 Chartres Street. The story goes that Corrado Giacona was pressured by the mafia to pay protection money, but he refused. Instead, he fortified his house by installing bolted doors and placing bars in the windows. Corrado also gave revolvers to each of his family members and taught them how to shoot. One night in 1909, Corrado and his family were eating dinner when four armed men entered the house through the upstairs gallery. Immediately, the Giaconas opened fire, killing three of the criminals and wounding one, who managed to escape. Several other attacks were made on the Giacona family's house before they finally moved out in the early 1920s. In 1925, the Beauregard Memorial Association prevented the new owner from converting the house into a macaroni factory. The association could not, however, save the adjoining garden.

In 1945, Beauregard's former home was purchased by author Frances Parkinson Keyes. While living there, she wrote novels in which two of the former owners were characters, P.G.T. Beauregard and Paul Morphy. She also restored the house and worked with the Garden-Study Club to replant the garden. Today, the Beauregard-Keyes house is a museum showcasing items that belonged to Beauregard and his wife and to Frances Parkinson Keyes. It is open for tours.

Rumors of the haunting of the Beauregard-Keyes surfaced in the years following World War II. Neighbors and passersby reported hearing the clash of swords, screams of wounded men, sounds of pistols and muskets and the booming of cannons coming from the house and the gardens. A few witnesses claimed to have seen the bloody bodies of the murderous intruders killed by the Giacona family. Some experts in the paranormal believe that the Civil War and the shooting of the Mafiosi left a psychic imprint on the house. Another legend concerns P.G.T. Beauregard and his wife. Because they were unable to hold a ball in the house, their ghosts return to the ballroom occasionally to host the gala event that never took place. The story is lent some validity by the experience of a girl who rented the apartment below the ballroom. In the morning, she complained of being unable to sleep because she was kept awake by the sound of music and the scraping of furniture in the ballroom. Author Troy Taylor claims that the house is also haunted by the ghost of a cat named Caroline and a cocker spaniel named Lucky. For years, tour guides and directors of the Beauregard have dismissed the reports of ghostly activity inside the historic home.

THE LABRANCHE HOUSE

New Orleans

According to the Louisiana State Tourist Commission, the LaBranche House at the corner of Royal and St. Peter Streets is the second most photographed building in the French Quarter, primarily because of its ornate lacework iron balconies. The property on which it stands was originally purchased by a free woman of color named Marianne Dubreui in 1796. Earlier structures on the site were destroyed by the fires of 1788 and 1794. In 1832, a rich sugar planter named Jean Baptiste LaBranche bought the property and constructed the three-story building that now stands there. His wife, Marie, added the wrought-iron balconies in 1843. Paul Napoleon bought the LaBranche House in 1869. For the remainder of the nineteenth century and into the twentieth century, thirty different people owned the historic structure. In the mid-twentieth century, the first floor of the building was converted into an Italian restaurant called Tortorici's. Famous for its veal, scampi and fish, Tororici's was one of the longest-running restaurants in New Orleans. In 2005, Tororici's closed following Hurricane Katrina. In 2008, the Ammari brothers bought the restaurant, restored the historic building and reopened the as the Royal Café. Most tourists and locals are drawn to the Royal Café for its atmosphere and Cajun and Creole cuisine. Some people, though, are intrigued by the stories that previous owners passed down for over a century.

The most persistent legend concerns Marie LaBranche and her husband's mistress. After her husband died, Marie was consumed with a desire to learn the identity of the young woman Jean Baptiste had been seeing on the side. After a great deal of effort, Marie found out who the woman was and where she lived. One night, Marie kidnapped her and brought her back to the house. She dragged the woman up the stairs and chained her to a wall in the attic. Marie then shut the door and left her husband's mistress to starve to death upstairs.

The paranormal presences inside the LaBranche House remained dormant, for the most part, until the building was remodeled in 2008. Marie LaBranche manifests as a woman in a dark blue dress with long, styled hair. She seems to enjoy interrupting the meals of diners by standing over their shoulder and staring down at them. Her nemesis is a restless spirit who is active on the third floor, where she moves tables and chairs around. She is also credited with throwing a coffee cup across the sales manager's desk. Her ghost seems to be determined to let people know that she died here in a horrible way.

Marie LaBranche is said to have starved her husband's mistress to death in the attic of the LaBranche House, one of the most photographed buildings in the French Quarter. *Alan Brown.*

Some of the disturbances in the LaBranche House have not been attributed to a specific ghost. Guests and staff have encountered cold spots inside the building. Lights turn off and on by themselves. Computers turn on and off at odd times. Doors open and close. Disembodied footsteps echo through the hallways. The psychic memory of the tragic event that occurred within the walls of the LaBranche House shows no signs of vanishing anytime soon.

THE JACKSON HOTEL

New Orleans

In the late 1700s, when New Orleans was devastated by outbreaks of yellow fever, fire and floods, hundreds of orphaned children wandered the streets, hungry and alone. They found refuge in places like an orphanage/school that once stood at 913 Royal Street. In August 1794, a fierce hurricane swept into

New Orleans from Cuba, damaging the orphanage, along with many other buildings in the city. In December 1794, a fire ravaged the city, destroying the orphanage. Five boys are said to have died in the conflagration. When the debris was cleared, a courthouse was built in its place. It is remembered today for the trial of Andrew Jackson. After the Battle of New Orleans in 1815, he maintained martial law, requiring people who had been accused of a crime to stand before a military tribunal. When a man named Louis Louallier wrote a letter to the newspaper demanding the martial law be lifted, Jackson threw him in jail. Jackson was ordered by U.S. District Court judge Dominick Hall to free Louallier, but Jackson drove Hall out of the city instead. Hall returned to the courtroom after martial law was lifted and charged Jackson with contempt of court. During the trial, Jackson refused to answer questions and was fined $1,000. Ironically, the crowd waiting outside of the courthouse proclaimed him a hero. They even raised $1,000 to pay his fine. He asked them to give the money to the families of the thirteen Americans who died in the Battle of New Orleans. The courthouse was abandoned in the 1840s and was eventually torn down. In 1888, a one-story boarding house with an inner courtyard was built on the site. After a second story was added, the structure became the Jackson Hotel.

The Jackson Hotel is one of the city's best-known haunted locations. Some of the hauntings date to the years when a courthouse stood on the site. One of these ghosts is the forlorn figure of a man. His hands are tied behind his back, and his head is bowed, as if he is standing before a judge who had just pronounced a sentence. The hotel's most illustrious ghost is the spirit of Andrew Jackson, who appears to have a strong connection to the site of his public vindication.

Most of the ghosts that frequent the Jackson Hotel are the spirits of little boys, possibly the children who died in the fire. They are playful spirits who enjoy playing in the inner courtyard and running down the hallways in the dead of night. Guests and staff have heard small voices and light footsteps in unexpected parts of the hotel. Their piercing screams echo through the halls, as well. In her book *Haunted New Orleans*, author Bonny Stuart reports that the manager recalled seeing little boys pass through the walls. He even saw the tops of their small heads as they attempted to peer over the lobby counter.

One of the most disturbing encounters with the ghost children of the Jackson Hotel took place in the 1980s. A man and woman who were visiting New Orleans booked a room in the hotel. They spent the day sightseeing, dining at restaurants and shopping at the city's plethora of gift shops. Late

The Jackson Hotel is said to be haunted by the ghosts of children who perished in a fire. *Alan Brown.*

that night, the exhausted couple returned to the hotel. They placed their camera and bags of merchandise on the dresser, changed their clothes and went to bed. They returned home the next day and took the film from their camera to the local drugstore to be developed. As they looked through the photographs, they were shocked to find the image on the very last one: someone appeared to have taken a picture of them sleeping in their bed in the Jackson Hotel. At that moment, the fanciful stories the manager had told them about the hotel's mischievous little ghosts became very real.

THE BOURBON ORLEANS HOTEL

New Orleans

The Bourbon Orleans Hotel originated as the Theatre d'Orleans. Plans for the theater designed in the French-Provincial style had been made in 1806, but construction was not completed until 1815, due to the War of 1812. One year after it was built, the Theatre d'Orleans was destroyed by fire. It was rebuilt by a refugee from Saint-Domingue named John Davis. Encouraged by the success of the theater, Davis built an addition—the Salle d'Orleans (Orleans Ballroom). The ballroom soon became the center of social life in Creole society. Countless balls were held here, including the quadroon balls, which provided mistresses for wealthy men. During the Civil War, which virtually put an end to nightlife in New Orleans, the popularity of the theater and the ballroom declined. In 1881, the Sisters of the Holy Family, the first Black convent, transformed the former Salle d'Orleans into a chapel. For eighty-three years, the former theater and ballroom served as an orphanage, a convent and the first Catholic school for Black girls in New Orleans. At one time, four hundred nuns and more than 1,300 students called the academy home. In the 1960s, the Bourbon Kings Hotel Corporation purchased the building, which had fallen into disrepair, and undertook a massive restoration project. Today, the Bourbon Orleans is one of the city's most popular luxury hotels with all of the amenities, including a fitness center, a heated outdoor saltwater pool, free Wi-Fi and 218 guest rooms, some of which are rumored to be haunted.

Seventeen ghosts are said to haunt the Bourbon Orleans Hotel, which has become a popular stop on local ghost tours. One of the most haunted places inside the hotel is the Orleans Ballroom, which has become a venue

The structure that became the Bourbon Orleans Hotel was built on the site of the Theatre d'Orleans after it was destroyed by fire. *Alan Brown.*

for weddings, receptions and meetings. In the nineteenth century, it is said that the ballroom hosted quadroon balls. They were an outgrowth of plaçage, which was an extralegal system through which ethnic European men entered into liaisons with women of African and Native American descent. Many of these "mulatto courtesans" met their clients at these quadroon balls, the first of which was organized in 1805 by Albert Tessier at an early incarnation of the Bourbon Orleans Hotel. Most of these young women attended these dances in the hope of becoming the mistress of a rich young Creole gentleman. Once a quadroon woman attracted an admirer's attention, her mother usually negotiated the compensation for setting up the arrangement. The ghost of one of these beautiful young women has been sighted dancing by herself beneath the chandelier. A spectral figure hiding behind the curtains is said to be responsible for the rustling sound reported by guests, staff and even owners of the hotel on days when none of the windows are open.

A bloodstain on the ballroom carpet harkens to the days when love-starved Creoles vied for the charms of young women at balls. When tempers flared,

The Orleans Ballroom, which hosted quadroon balls in the nineteenth century, is said to be haunted by the apparition of a beautiful young woman who dances under the crystal chandelier. *Alan Brown.*

some of these gentlemen settled their differences by dueling at St. Anthony's Garden behind St. Louis Cathedral. According to legend, a young man who was wounded in one of these duels rushed back to the ballroom and bled on the floor. The bloodstain has resisted all efforts to remove it.

According to visitors and employees, one of the former nuns who lived on the property has never left. Guests in room 644 report seeing the spectral figure of a nun standing over their beds. People who have seen her sense that the nun is watching over them. She is said to be the spirit of a nun who committed suicide in the convent. The mournful cries that have been heard in the room seem to confirm this legend.

The ghosts of children have been sighted in the Bourbon Orleans Hotel, as well. Children who were orphaned by the yellow fever epidemic in 1853 found shelter in the orphanage at St. Mary's Academy. The number of children in the orphanage increased considerably after the yellow fever epidemic of 1878. A number of orphans succumbed to the disease, despite the nuns' efforts to keep them safe. Their playful presence has livened the hotel for over a century. Waitstaff attribute the sudden shaking of tables and

The ghosts of orphans who perished in the yellow fever epidemic of 1878 haunt the hallways of the Bourbon Orleans Hotel. *Alan Brown.*

glasses to the antics of the ghost children. People walking down the hallways have encountered cold spots, often accompanied by childish laughter. Small, unseen hands have been known to yank at the back of guests' shirts. The apparition of a little girl running after a ball down the sixth-floor corridor has been seen many times over the years.

A more sober spectral personage is the ghost of one of the Confederate soldiers who attempted to prevent Union troops from capturing New Orleans in 1862. He is possibly one of many wounded soldiers who died in one of the field hospitals scattered throughout the city. Eyewitnesses describe the soldier as wearing a homespun uniform. He stands at attention with blood seeping from his open wounds. Many employees at the hotel believe he is the ghost whose weary footsteps resound through the hallways on the third and sixth floors, dragging his sword on the marble floors.

THE LALAURIE HOUSE

New Orleans

Many of New Orleans's ghost legends are tinged with violence and murder. Some of these crimes are generated by the clash between the city's wide variety of cultures. Crimes of passion have been memorialized in New Orleans lore. Undoubtedly, the most disturbing—and bizarre—murders are those that seem to have been committed for no apparent reason. Such is the case with the murders that took place in the city's most notorious haunted house, the Lalaurie House.

The age of the house at 1140 Royal Street is uncertain. According to one tradition, Jean and Henri de Remarie built the three-story mansion in 1173 on a site that they had acquired through a land grant from the French colonial government. Delphine de Macarty inherited the mansion before marrying her third husband, Dr. Leonard Louis Nicolas Lalaurie in 1825. However, legal records indicate that Edmond Soniat du Fossat sold the house to Louis and Delphine Lalaurie on August 13, 1831. Except for the delicate lace ironwork around the second-floor balcony, the exterior of the house is rather plain. The interior of the mansion, however, was much more elaborate, with its mahogany doors, hand-carved panels, marble floors and crystal chandeliers. The Lalaurie mansion was the ideal venue for Madame Lalaurie's lavish parties. She soon became one of the most influential members of Creole society. She and her guests were pampered by dozens of slaves, one of whom, a finely dressed butler, was always at Madame Lalaurie's side.

Before long, though, rumors began circulating around New Orleans regarding Delphine Lalaurie's mistreatment of her slaves. Several of them appeared to be shockingly gaunt and hollow-eyed. A neighbor remarked that several of her slaves, such as the parlor maid and the stable boy, appeared to have disappeared for no apparent reason. Madame Lalaurie's abuse of her slaves received some credibility when several witnesses saw her chasing her personal maid, a seven-year-old girl across the third-floor roof of the house, brandishing a whip. Suddenly, the child jumped off the steep roof and struck the pavestones below, barely missing someone passing by. Locals whispered to each other that desperation drove the girl to commit suicide. One woman said that the girl was buried beneath the cypress trees in the yard. The publicity of the incident compelled the authorities to investigate the stories people were telling about the Lalauries. Ultimately, Delphine

Built by Marie Delphine MacCarthy Blanque Lalaurie in 1832, the building, known as the Haunted House, was the site of unspeakable horrors. *Alan Brown.*

Lalaurie was forced to sell all of her slaves. However, some of her relatives bought them and sold them back to the Lalauries.

The horrible truth of the secrets harbored in the mansion was revealed one day when clouds of fire and smoke billowed from a window. With surprising calm, Delphine instructed the firefighters to remove the expensive furnishings. When the firefighters arrived, throngs of bystanders were milling around in front of the Lalaurie House. One of the neighbors, Montreuil, inquired about the welfare of the slaves, but Madame Lalaurie told him to mind his own business. The man then expressed his concerns to a local judge standing in the crowd, and he instructed the firefighters to check out the entire house. They traced the origin of the fire to the kitchen. It had been set by a cook who was chained to the stove. As the men were releasing her, she pointed to a door leading to the garret and said, "Go up there."

What they found in the attic haunted their dreams for the rest of their lives. One dozen naked slaves, male and female, were chained to the walls, strapped to operating tables and locked in cages. The floor was littered with human appendages. Buckets were filled with human organs. One man dangling from his chains had a stick protruding from his skull. Someone seemed to have "stirred his brains" around in his head. One of the men's amputated hands had been sewn to his stomach. Some of the men had their eyes gouged out, their fingernails removed, their mouths pinned shut and their ears sliced off. Several of the woman were lying down with their intestines wrapped around their waists. One woman whose limbs had been broken had been placed in a small cage. When she was released, she looked more like a crab than a human being. Many of the people were covered in maggots. Several corpses were strewn across the floorboards in various states of decay. The survivors were transported to the Cabildo, where they received food and water and treatment for their wounds. No one knows for sure the exact number of slaves who were victimized by the Lalauries. Spectators who had congregated to see the brutalized slaves seethed with anger.

At the same time, an angry mob was taking shape outside of the house at 1103 Royal Street. People were yelling and screaming and shaking their fists at the window. Suddenly, at the hour when Delphine usually took her carriage ride around the French Quarter, the doors to the courtyard were thrown open, and a carriage rattled into the mob at full speed. Some people dived out of the way, while others exclaimed, "Shoot her! Stop the carriage! Shoot the horses!" The fate of Madame Lalaurie is uncertain. Some people believe she caught a ship that took her to Paris, where she spent the rest of her days in a splendid mansion. Others say that she hurried down Bayou Road, where she settled in a home under the name the Widow Blanque.

Reports of paranormal activity inside the Lalaurie House began soon after Madame Lalaurie's hasty exit from New Orleans. Not long after the mansion was sacked by the outraged citizens of New Orleans, people passing by the empty house on the sidewalk claimed to have heard screams and moans coming from the second floor. In 1837, a man purchased the house but was unable to live there because of the unnerving sounds. He tried leasing it out, but his renters could not live there either.

The Lalaurie House stood abandoned until 1874, when it was converted into an integrated high school. The White League forced the school to close. The segregationist school board reopened it as school for Black children, but it closed after a year. In 1882, the former Lalaurie House was temporarily restored to its former position as a social center for high society when it became a school of music and dancing. The school closed, though, just before a dance recital because of the dance instructor's alleged improprieties with some of the young ladies.

In the late 1880s, the house's tragic legacy continued when a wealthy eccentric named Jules Vigne secretly moved into the infamous house. In 1892, his ragged corpse was found lying on a cot. He had apparently been living in filth for years, even though a bag containing hundreds of dollars was nearby. Even more puzzling was the discovery of a hoard of valuable antiques in one of the rooms. Once again, the house was abandoned.

In the late 1890s, the now dilapidated Lalaurie House became a boarding house for Italian immigrants. Like others who had lived there before, the apartment dwellers found it impossible to remain there for very long. One boarder claimed that he was attacked during the night by the ghost of a Black man in chains. Small children were chased by the ghost of a woman with a whip. A young mother was shocked to see the ghostly figure of a well-dressed woman standing over her sleeping child. Phantom screams and moans made it difficult to sleep at night.

After standing vacant for a while, the house was turned into a bar called the Haunted Bar for a short while, before it became a furniture store. One morning shortly after the store opened, the owner discovered that the furniture was covered in blood, feces and urine. At first, he suspected that vandals had done the damage. The second time it happened, the store owner closed the store.

Over the next fifty years, the Lalaurie house passed through a number of different incarnations. In 1923, the old building was home to Warrington

House, where poverty-stricken men, many of whom had just been released from jail or prison, found refuge. Nine years later, the Grand Consistory of Louisiana moved into the Lalaurie Mansion and remained there until 1942. In 1969, the former residence was converted into an apartment building. In the 1970s and 1980s, the historic home underwent two restorations under the guidance of the architectural firm of Koch and Wilson. One of the house's most famous occupants was Nicholas Cage, who bought the Lalaurie House in April 2007 for $3.45 million. He said that he bought the house because he believed it would inspire him to write the great American horror novel. However, Cage had not written very much before he was forced to sell the house to the Birmingham, Alabama–based Regions Bank for $2.5 million in November 2009. Today, the Lalaurie is still a private residence. Even though it is not open to the public, the Lalaurie House has become a regular stop on the city's haunted tours. Between October 9, 2013, and January 29, 2014, Kathy Bates played Delphine Lalaurie in the television series *American Horror Story: Coven.*

On June 7, 2019, the Syfy Channel program *Portals to Hell* broadcast the first televised paranormal investigation of the Lalaurie Mansion. The show opened with hosts Jack Osborne and Katrina Weidman's interview with a woman named Annie Elsas, who lived at the Lalaurie Mansion with her family between 1963 and 1964. Annie said that they were unaware of the house's reputation before they moved. Not long after they moved in, the beds in one of the rooms were shoved to the middle of the floor. As time passed, Annie was awakened by the sounds of screams in the middle of the night. Eventually, she had to sleep with a night light because of all the nocturnal disturbances. One day, Annie was standing outside of the house when she saw the figure of a little Black girl sitting on a corner of the roof of the house. When Annie returned to the house in the 1980s, she was knocked down by an invisible force. At the end of the interview, Annie said, "It haunts me. It never left me."

Jack and Katrina's next interview was with Lisa Hadley, the housekeeper. She no longer lives at the house, but her mother, the caretaker, does. Lisa said that one day her cousin sent her a fax from the Lalaurie house that read, "Hi Lisa." When Lisa received the message, it read, "Hi. I'm Madame Lalaurie." Hadley said that one day she entered the dining room and saw a little girl in a white outfit looking out the window. One of her most unnerving experiences occurred when an invisible hand touched her in the slave quarters. Lisa added that an electrician who works at the house has had strange experiences. One afternoon, something hit him the head while he was in the attic. Carol, Lisa's mother, said that she does not like being in the kitchen on the second floor because the door leading to the servants' quarters tends to slam shut on its own.

Jack and Katrina's investigation of the house began in Annie's former bedroom at 10:05 p.m. Not long after they started, a voice, saying, "There are nine people in the room," came through the Geoport device. It turned out that there actually were nine investigators in the room at the time. When Katrina asked the entity if it died at the hands of Madame Lalaurie and if it was the spirit of the little girl that Annie saw, it responded, "Yes" to both questions.

The investigation then moved to the slave quarters. Within a few minutes, Jack saw a shadow move across a picture. Then all of the investigators heard a deep growling sound. When Jack asked the entity if it was Madame Lalaurie, a voice responded, "Yes."

All at once, Jack exclaimed, "There's a shadow walking across the reflection of lights on one of the walls." Then the photographer said that something was blocking the lights on her camera. In an effort to communicate with the spirits further, Jack and Katrina took out a Ouija board and asked, "Are there spirits in this room?" Almost instantly, they heard a knocking sound in a corner.

The group split up for the next phase of the investigation. Katrina and Elaine, the producer, went into the attic. Using the Geoport, Katrina and Elaine heard a voice say, "Lot of hurt."

Meanwhile, Jack heard another knock when he asked, "Were you a slave here and were you tortured here?" The next question provoked the most unsettling response. Jack asked, "Do you want us to leave?" and the response was, "Yes." Jack and his partner left immediately.

The next day, Jack confirmed that the Lalaurie House was indeed haunted. The most haunted part of the house was the slave quarters. "There are leftover spirits here from a highly traumatic event," he said.

THE MYRTLES

St. Francisville

After spending several days at the Myrtles in St. Francisville, Louisiana, representatives of the Smithsonian Institute declared it the most haunted house in America. Revolutionary War general David Bradford built the Myrtles in the Creole cottage style on 650 acres that he had received as part of a land grant in 1796. For six years, he occupied himself by growing cotton and indigo on the plantation. After President John Adams pardoned Bradford for his participation in the Whiskey Rebellion, his wife, Elizabeth, and their five children moved to St. Francisville from Pennsylvania. Elizabeth took over the day-to-day operation of the plantation after her husband died in 1808. In 1817, she turned over management of the plantation to her daughter Mathilda and her husband, Clarke Woodruff. They inherited the Myrtles after Elizabeth died in 1831, and they sold the plantation to Ruffin Gray Stirling in 1834. Stirling and his wife, Mary Catherine Cobb, extensively renovated the plantation house, making additions that doubled its size. They named it the Myrtles after the crepe myrtles that grew on the property. The Myrtles survived the Civil War relatively unscathed. In 1865, Mary Cobb Sterling's son-in-law, a lawyer named William Winter, became manager of the plantation. Financial setbacks forced the Winter

Considered by many parapsychologists to be the most haunted house in America, the Myrtles was built in 1796 by General David Bradford on 650 acres of land that he had acquired as part of a land grant. *Alan Brown.*

family to sell the Myrtles in 1868, but they were able to buy it back in 1870. William Winter was shot by a disgruntled client at the Myrtles in 1871. He died as he tried to climb up the stairs. In 1880, Mary Cobb Sterling's son Stephen inherited the plantation. The Myrtles passed out of the family when Stephen sold it to Oran D. Brooks in 1886. For the next ninety years, the plantation had a succession of different owners. In the 1970s, James and Frances Kermeen Meyers turned the Myrtles into a bed-and-breakfast. At the time of this writing, the Myrtles is owned by John and Teeta Moss.

At least twelve ghosts are said to haunt the Myrtles. Many people believe that the land Bradford received from the Spanish was cursed because it was a Tunecah Indian burial ground. The Native American link to the property could explain why the ghost of a beautiful Indian maiden has been seen inside the gazebo. The most often told legend concerns an enslaved woman named Chloe, who was owned by Clarke and Sara Woodruff. One day, Chloe was eavesdropping on a conversation Clarke was having with several of his friends in the gentlemen's parlor. When Woodruff saw her peeking through the keyhole, he jumped from his chair, dragged her outside and cut off one of her ears. To hide her disfigurement, Chloe began wearing a green turban. Determined to be restored to his good graces, she decided to mix oleander with the batter of a birthday cake she was baking for one of Sara's three daughters. She thought that if she added just enough oleander to make them sick, she could nurse them back to health and prove her worth to the family. Unfortunately, she miscalculated, and Sara and two of the little girls died. Frantic, Chloe ran outside and told the other slaves what she had done. Knowing that Chloe had committed an unpardonable crime, they hanged her from a tree to prevent blame from falling on their heads.

Though no record of Chloe's existence has ever been found, stories of a green-turbaned ghost roaming the plantation at night have persisted for over a century. Years ago, a photograph taken of the exterior of the house captured the blurry image of a woman with a turban between the main house and the former kitchen. Guests have sworn that they have been tucked in at night by a woman wearing a turban. Frances Kermeen Meyers said that in 1987, she was sleeping in a first-floor bedroom when she was woken by a Black woman in a dark gown holding a candle. She vanished as soon as Frances started screaming. The fact that the woman was wearing a turban convinced Frances that she had had an encounter with Chloe.

The young children who died in the house were victims of disease, not murder. One of them was eight-year-old Kate Sterling, who contracted yellow fever. Her parents were so desperate for a cure that they enlisted

William Winter fell on the seventeenth step of the staircase and died in his wife's arms after being shot by a disgruntled client in 1871. A thudding sound is occasionally heard on the step where he died. *Alan Brown.*

the aid of a voodoo priestess from a nearby plantation. Despite her incantations, the child died in her father's arms in what is now the William Winter Room. Legend has it that the priestess was hanged for failing to save the little girl's life.

A number of other ghosts have also made appearances at the Myrtles. The ghosts of Woodruff's two murdered daughters have been seen playing on the grounds. Tour guide Hester Erbe was certain that the spectral woman who walked down the stairs behind her was Sara, the mother of the murdered little girls. A thudding sound is occasionally heard on the seventeenth step of the staircase where William Winter fell and died in his wife's arms. A Confederate soldier who was brought to the Myrtles when it served as a field hospital has been seen lying in a bed in one of the rooms. A second Confederate soldier marches up and down the front porch. There is a ghost of a thin young man in a colorful vest, Ruffin Grey Sterling's son, who was stabbed over a gambling debt and dropped dead in the dining room. His ghost has been seen in one of the upper rooms. Women sleeping by themselves have had the feeling that someone was sleeping next to them. Their suspicions were confirmed the next morning

The spirits of Sarah Woodruff and her children are said to be trapped inside this antique mirror in the Myrtles. *Marilyn Brown.*

by the impression of a body next to them in the bed. The sprits of Sarah Woodruff and her children are said to be trapped inside the full-length mirror because the mirror was not covered after their death. Scratches on the mirror and a smudge that appears to be the handprint of a child are accepted by some as proof of their captivity. Tourists and employees have also seen the ghost of a young girl who appears just before thunderstorms and the spirit of a French person who wanders from one room to the next. Some people believe there is a ghost in the Myrtles who sits at the piano and plays the same chord repeatedly.

My wife, Marilyn, and I spent two nights at the Myrtles in July 2012. When we arrived in the late afternoon, we carried our bags to the second floor of the main house. We stayed in the William Winters Room, where Kate Sterling had died of yellow fever. Before we unpacked our suitcases, I took pictures of the room, hoping to "catch" something on my camera. When I looked at a photograph I had taken of a large chair by the rear wall, I noticed that my wife's image was clearly visible in the full-length mirror behind it. Without moving, I asked her to stand aside, and I took another photograph from the same position. I was surprised—and, of course, delighted—to find a large orb in the seat of the chair that I had just photographed about one minute earlier.

This was not the only paranormal experience we had at the Myrtles that weekend. That night, we were sitting in the courtyard having a drink, when my wife decided to take a photograph of the fountain. When she looked at the photo, she exclaimed, "Alan, look at this!" There, right in front of the fountain, was a large misty shape that was not visible with the naked eye. I immediately grabbed my camera and took a picture from the same spot. The mist was gone.

We were not the only guests who had strange experiences that night. One gentleman told us that he was walking around the grounds taking pictures the previous afternoon, and in a photograph of the gazebo was a misty shape. A woman and her daughter who stayed in the room down from us said that they had set their luggage on the floor and went to town for lunch.

Left: During my stay in the William Winter Room, where little Kate Sterling died of yellow fever, I captured the image of an orb. Nothing appeared in the first photograph I took of the chair. *Alan Brown.*

Right: My wife captured this image of a ghostly mist hovering around the fountain in the courtyard at the Myrtles. *Marilyn Brown.*

The specter of a beautiful Native American maiden has been seen standing inside the gazebo, possibly because the Myrtles was rumored to have been built on Native American burial ground. *Alan Brown.*

When they returned, they were shocked to find that over half of a roll of toilet paper had been unrolled and was lying all over the bathroom floor and in the main room. On the morning of the second day, Marilyn and I were in the former kitchen when a guest walked up to Teta Moss and complained that some earrings she had placed on the dresser before she went to bed were not there when she woke. Teta replied that several guests had the same experience in that room. The best explanation that she could come up with was that Chloe's ghost appears to have a fondness for jewelry and occasionally takes it from guest rooms and hides it in the yard. Over the years, several pieces of jewelry have been found next to trees and under large rocks. Teta took the lady's name and address and promised to return the earrings as soon as they turned up.

Marilyn and I left the Myrtles convinced more than ever that there are some things in this world that cannot be fully explained by logic. I must say that for Marilyn and me, the Myrtles certainly lived up to its reputation. My healthy skepticism was still firmly in place, but it had been chipped away considerably after that weekend in America's most haunted house.

THE HAUNTED HOUMA BRIDGE

Houma

Built in 1962, the Houma Navigation Bridge spans the Houma Navigation Canal on LA 661. Its total length is 262 feet, and its deck width is 23.9 feet. Houma bridge has an average daily traffic of 9,500 cars. It is an important part of the lives of the residents of Houma, not only because of the memories they have of crossing it throughout their lives but also because of the strange stories people tell about it.

The accidents that have occurred on the bridge have generated a number of ghost stories. Some say it is haunted by the spirit of a woman who died in an automobile accident in the tunnel years ago. Her apparition is usually seen at night inside the bridge. Many people hold their breath as they pass over the intracoastal waterway, possibly to keep from inhaling evil spirits. Another popular legend concerns a water spirit that haunts the bridge. It is said that if anyone mocks the spirit or expresses disbelief, the car will have some sort of water damage.

In recent years, many people have argued for replacing the Houma Bridge with an overpass. The reasons include high maintenance costs and traffic jams. One must wonder, though, if the bridge's ghostly reputation is another reason why people want it razed.

4.

LEGENDARY OUTLAWS

The Death of Bonnie and Clyde

Gibsland

On May 23, 1934, Bonnie Parker and Clyde Barrow were driving a stolen Ford Deluxe on a lonely backroad in Beienville Parish, near Gibsland, Louisiana. Unknown to them, six men were hiding in the bushes—Texas officers Frank Hamer, Hinton Alcorn and B.M. "Maney" Gault and Louisiana officers Henderson Jordan and Prentiss Morel Oakley. Each officer had a shotgun, a rifle and pistols. Just a few yards down from the policemen was a relative of one of the members of the Barrow gang. The officers had persuaded him to stand by his truck and pretend that it had stalled. As soon as Clyde Barrow pulled off the road to help the man, all six officers began firing before the couple could climb out of the car. According to one account, one of the men yelled, "Halt!" before opening fire. Another account has it that one of the youngest officers, probably Oakley, started firing first. One of the policemen guessed that they had fired over 150 rounds. According to another account, 167 shots were fired. Bonnie and Clyde did not have time to fire a single shot. He was killed instantly by a shot to the head; Bonnie, however, screamed as the bullets mowed her down. Years later, one of the officers said that Bonnie's screams haunted him for the rest of his life. Afterward, the coroner reported that Clyde had been shot seventeen

Part of the myth of Bonnie and Clyde as a pair of carefree lovers can be traced to the photographs they took of themselves. *Wikimedia Commons.*

times and that Bonnie had been shot twenty-six times. Supposedly, they had been shot so many times that the embalming fluid leaked out of the bullet holes. One police officer described their mutilated bodies as "a bunch of wet rags." Bonnie and Clyde's two-year crime spree had come to a bloody end.

News of the deaths of Bonnie and Clyde spread to Gibsland not long after the last shot was fired. The officers recalled souvenir hunters cutting off pieces of the couple's clothing. One woman cut off bloody locks of Bonnie's hair. A man even tried to cut off Clyde's ear. Others were picking up shell casings and shards of broken glass from the roadside. Once they had secured the area, the police towed the car with the bodies inside to the Conger Furniture Store and Funeral Parlor in Acadia, Louisiana. Within hours, the population of the town swelled from two thousand to between twelve and sixteen thousand, all hoping to catch a glimpse of the bullet-ridden car and the bullet-ridden bodies inside. An undertaker named H.D. Darby and a real estate agent named Sophia Stone were summoned from nearby Ruston, Louisiana, to identify the bodies because both of them had been kidnapped by Bonnie and Clyde earlier. Prophetically, Bonnie pronounced that Darby might "work on her" someday.

The bodies were then transported to Texas for public viewings. An estimated ten thousand people viewed Clyde's body; Bonnie's mother guessed that around twenty thousand people walked past her daughter's corpse. So many people attended the funerals that Clyde's pallbearers found it difficult to carry the coffin through the crowd of onlookers. Although Bonnie had written a poem predicting that she and Clyde would be buried together, her mother did not respect her daughter's last wish. Bonnie was buried in Fishtrap Cemetery first and then moved to Crown Hill memorial Park in Dallas in 1945. Clyde was interred next to his brother in Western Heights Cemetery in Dallas.

The aftermath of Bonnie and Clyde's deaths and funerals is equally fascinating. For years, the death car was displayed at amusement parks, fairs and flea markets. For a while, patrons could even sit inside the car for the price of one dollar. The death car, as well as the bloody shirt Clyde was wearing, was displayed at the Primm Valley Resort and Casino in Nevada before being moved to a casino called Whiskey Pete's in Prim. The American National Insurance Company of Galveston, Texas, paid the insurance policies in full for Bonnie and Clyde. The Ambush Site Marker is located eight miles south of Gibsland on Highway 154. Its pock-marked face has been chipped away by souvenir hunters. In Gibsland, one can find the Bonnie and Clyde Ambush Museum. It was operated by "Boots" Hinton, a son of one of the

Located eight miles from Bonnie and Clyde's ambush site, the Bonnie and Clyde Ambush Museum in Gibsland was owned and operated by Boots Hinton, the son of one of the men who killed the couple. *Wikimedia Commons.*

lawmen who killed Bonnie and Clyde, until his death in 2016. The museum is housed in an old restaurant, Ma Canfield's Café, where Bonnie and Clyde bought two breakfast sandwiches to go. Legend has it that Bonnie was holding her half-eaten sandwich when she was killed. Inside the museum is a bullet-ridden 1934 Ford Deluxe V-8, bloody mannequins representing Bonnie and Clyde and one of Clyde's Remington shotguns.

THE WEST-KIMBRELL GANG

Winn Parish

Formed in 1806, the Neutral Zone extended over five thousand square miles from the Calcasieu River on the west to the Sabine River on the east. Natchitoches, its northern border, stretched all the way to the Gulf of

Mexico. The Neutral Zone, which served as a buffer between the Spanish and American territories, was a haven for outlaws in the early nineteenth century because the of the absence of government. One of these outlaws was John West, who fled to the Neutral Zone after murdering a man. West settled in Atlanta, Louisiana, in Winn Parish. He fought for the Confederacy during the Civil War, and when he returned to Louisiana, he was outraged to find that carpetbaggers had been victimizing the residents of his state. Around 1866, West made the acquaintance of another Confederate veteran, Jackson Laws Kimbrell, who also lived in Atlanta and shared West's opinion of carpetbaggers. The two men formed a home guard, whose mission was to protect citizens from people who felt they were above the law. The home guard in its outward form comprised the most upstanding members of the community, such as ministers and church members. The home guard's inner circle, however, included thieves and murderers, who, in many ways, were worse than the "lawbreakers" they were supposed to be protecting the community from. The first victim of the nightriders, as they came to be known, was a Union paymaster, Simeon G. Butts. In 1866, Butts was shot and robbed of $2,700.

The West-Kimbrell Gang's modus operandi was simple. Travelers were invited to spend the night at the home of one of the gang members. While they were sleeping, the owner of the house crept into the bedroom, knocked them on the head and stole all of their possessions. They got rid of the bodies of men, women and children by throwing them down a well. Over time, they killed so many people that they had to dig a well every mile along a forty-mile stretch of the Harrisonburg Road. Witnesses to their crimes were killed as well. Gang members communicated with each other through the use of Chickasaw tree marks.

In 1870, a member of the West-Kimbrell Gang, whose name is unknown, rode up to the house of his cousin Jim Carter. He invited Carter to accompany him to a house in Cedar Bluff, where a party was being held. When the two men rode up to the house, the rough appearance of the men inside convinced Jim that they were not there to party. Carter was told that he was being admitted into the clan and that he would be expected to murder women, children and infants and hide their bodies. Fearing death if he refused, Carter agreed. That night, Carter was able to sneak out of the house and ride back home. Hot on his heels was his cousin, who was brandishing a pistol. When the man stopped to water his horse at a small creek, Carter aimed his pistol from his saddle and shot his cousin, staining the waters red with his blood.

The year 1872 spelled the beginning of the end for John West. A member of the clan named Dan Dean became embroiled in an argument with John West. He tried to kill Dean but was prevented from doing so by Laws Kimbrell. On Easter Sunday, 1872, West, who also served as deputy sheriff, "arrested" Dean's in-laws, taking them to the Masonic lodge and suspending them from the rafters by their thumbs. Filled with rage, Dean appealed to the governor, who offered full pardons to anyone who aided in the removal of the gang. A few months later, a group of vigilantes confronted members of West's gang in Atlanta. In just a few minutes, gunfire erupted. The blast of a shotgun removed West's head and propelled it to a fence post. Legend has it that West's head remained atop of that fencepost for many years. All of the gang members surrendered, except for Laws Kimbrell, who was offered clemency for helping save Dean's life during the gunfight. West's decapitated corpse, as well as the bodies of the gang members killed in the gun battle, was buried in the Methodist Cemetery in Atlanta. However, because of their evil deeds, some of the outlaws were buried standing up in the belief that their souls would never be at rest.

EUGENE BUNCH: THE GENTLEMAN TRAIN ROBBER

Franklinton

Over time, a number of American outlaws have been shrouded in a romantic aura. Jesse James had fully morphed into a folk hero by the time of his death. The same can be said of Probation-era outlaws Bonnie and Clyde. In the same league was Eugene Bunch. His was born in Mississippi, possibly in the late 1830s or early 1840s. During the Civil War, Bunch rose to the rank of captain while serving in Company E of the Third Louisiana Cavalry. After his release from the military, Bunch married a woman from Louisiana and began working as a schoolteacher. After a short time, the couple moved to Gainesville, Texas, where he became a newspaper editor. Some people believe that he became a train robber because of the gambling habit he picked up while living in Gainesville.

He eventually formed a gang with a few other bandits. Between 1888 and 1892, Bunch and his gang robbed six trains. Bunch became famous following his singlehanded robbery of the express car on the New Orleans and Northeastern Railway in 1889. It was said that his manner was gruff when he addressed the express car messengers, threatening to "blow their brains out" if they did not obey his commands. However, he always made his demands in a soft voice. When he robbed the passengers on the trains, he went under the name Captain J.F. Gerard. He was always gentlemanly in his treatment of the ladies. He took their money and jewels, but he tipped his hat and did not steal their handbags. He was respectful to the men, but he took their wallets.

An article published in the January 4, 1889 edition of the *Daily Picayune* presented a more personal profile of the outlaw. The article reveals Bunch's visit to Folsom's guns store, where he befriended the clerk, a gunsmith named William Geneate. The gunsmith described Bunch as "a man who had traveled extensively, was intelligent and well-educated and a very entertaining talker." At the time, Geneate assumed that Bunch was a cowboy because he was wearing a broad-brimmed, white felt hat. Bunch refused to impart any specifics about his activities, saying that he "was running between New Orleans and Texas." During this visit, Bunch presented Geneate with a .44-caliber single-action revolver that needed repairs. While he was working on the weapon, the mainspring broke. Instead of becoming angry, Bunch said he was glad the accident had happened because he would have been in a "bad fix" if the gun malfunctioned while he was using it. Bunch said he needed the mainspring fixed because he had a "shooting match" coming up. Geneate recalled that on a previous visit, Bunch had brought him a .38-caliber rifle that he wanted to be re-bored to a .40-caliber. Another time, Bunch brought in a telescopic sight that he wanted cleaned.

During the four years in which Bunch's gang robbed trains, their total haul amounted to more than $30,000. Bunch's largest robbery was also his last. After stealing $20,000 from a train in New Orleans, he was followed by a band of Pinkerton agents. They chased him and his men into a swamp. Shots were fired, and Bunch and his cohorts lay dead in the muck of the swamp. Eugene Bunch was buried in Franklinton, Louisiana.

LEATHER BRITCHES SMITH

Grabow

In the early 1900s, a timber war was waged between the lumber companies and the timber workers in the Piney Woods of Louisiana and eastern Texas. The large sawmill owners required that their workers take a loyalty oath, sign a noncompete clause and sign what were called Yellow Dog contracts, which prevented them from joining a union. Employees who broke the rules were blacklisted, making it impossible to find work at any other mills. In the event of a strike by unionized workers, strike breakers—nonunion workers—were brought in to take their places.

The timber war of 1911–12 culminated in the Grabow Riot. On July 7, 1912, fifteen wagonloads of union workers were on their way to Grabow. Arthur L. Emerson was heading the effort to organize sawmill workers. When the wagons arrived at the Grabow office at 3:30 p.m., gunfire erupted from all sides. Three men were killed and fifty were wounded. Fifty-eight workers were charged with murder or inciting riots. Most of the workers were acquitted.

One of the men involved in the shoot-out was a gunman named Charles "Leather Britches" Smith. He was hired by A.L. Emerson to provide protection for the workers. People say that he carried a rifle and wore two pistols. He had a reputation as a murderer and a scoundrel. However, some people said that he was a good man most of the time, except when he drank. When the shooting began, Smith ran into the woods. A posse was formed to track him down. The men finally caught up with Smith on September 25, 1912. The leader ordered Smith to surrender; Smith raised his rifle and was cut down in a hail of bullets. His body was transported to Merryville, where it was placed in a box loaded with ice. The box was leaned against the outside wall of the Merryville Jail. For almost the entire day, onlookers paraded past Smith's bullet-ridden corpse. Because the community was divided in its opinion of Smith, he was buried on the fence line of the Merryville Cemetery. The cedar board that marked his grave was replaced by a headstone in 2010.

Some people believed that Smith was actually Ben Myatt of Robertson County, Texas, who had murdered his wife. He was convicted and sentenced to hang in 1910, but he escaped from jail and fled to Louisiana. A Texas deputy disputed the claim that Smith and Myatt were the same man because they had different eye colors.

THE YOKUM GANG

Natchitoches Parish

The Yokum Gang was composed of Jesse Ray Yokum, his sons and some of his grandsons. Jesse Yokum was born in 1860 in Betetourt, Virginia. A veteran of the American Revolution, he started as a member of the Murrell, killing and robbing travelers along the Natchez Trace in western Mississippi. In the

1820s, Jesse Ray Yokum, his sons and some of his grandsons began stealing horses and slaves in Kentucky and in the Neutral Strip. Jesse Ray Yokum was tried in Natchitoches for murder and for bribing witnesses and jurors, but he was never convicted in a court of law. In 1822, Matthew Yokum proposed to Susan Callier. However, her father, Robert Callier, urged her to marry Charles Chandler. Interestingly enough, her uncle, James Callier, became a member of the Yokum after marrying a sister of one of the Yokum brothers. James Callier and Mathew Yokum killed Robert Callier and then traveled to San Augustine to murder Charles Chandler. However, Charles Chandler killed James Callier and Matthew Yokum with the help of a slave, who was also killed in the shoot-out.

The criminal activities of Jesse Yokum extended for three generations, from 1800 until 1878. One of the sons was hanged in Texas in 1841. Another son, Zach Yokum, was hanged by a band of "regulators" in Louisiana around 1876. One of Jesse Yokum's grandsons, Doc Addison, was fleeing a murder charge in Texas when he shot and killed four of the regulators who were chasing him. Several of the other members of the Yokum gang murdered a man who lived in Louisiana with his mixed-race wife and their children. The murderers' attempt to sell the man's family into slavery in Texas was foiled by David Renfroe, and his neighbors drove them out. The gang turned its sights on Pine Island Bayou in present-day Jefferson County, where they continued murdering and robbing the citizens of Louisiana. Once again, a group of vigilantes disrupted their criminal activities. They hanged Thomas Yokum and chased the other members out of the county. Local history tells us that the members of the Yokum family who embraced the criminal way of life were a small minority. Most of the Yokums were law-abiding citizens.

REVEREND DEVIL

Kisatchie

The outlaw who came to be known as the "Rob Roy of the Southwest" and the "Great Western Land Pirate" was born John Andrews Murrell in 1806 in Lunenberg County, Virginia, to Jeffrey Murrell and Zipha Andrews. His father was a Methodist circuit preacher. Ironically, three of his sons became petty thieves. As a boy, John Murrell moved to Williamson County, Tennessee, with his family. He committed his first crime at the age of seventeen, when he stole a horse. After spending a year in prison, Murrell got married and fathered children. Unfortunately, family life did nothing to quell his criminal tendencies. He continued to steal and make counterfeit money. He was sentenced to ten years hard labor in a Tennessee prison in 1834 for stealing a slave, whom he had planned to sell back to his enslaver. During his incarceration, Murrell reformed. Due to the unsanitary conditions inside the prison, Murrell contracted tuberculosis and was granted early release in 1844. Nine months after his release from prison, Murrell succumbed to the disease on November 1, 1844. Not long after Murrell was buried, his grave was vandalized. Parts of his body were stolen. His head was displayed at county fairs for many years. Although his skull disappeared long ago, one of his thumbs was acquired by the Tennessee State Museum.

These are the accepted facts of John Murrell's life, which became mired in myth with the publication of *A History of the Detection, Conviction, Lie and Designs of John A. Murel, the Great Western Land Pirate* by Virgil A. Stewart, writing under the pseudonym Augusts Q. Walton. Stewart claimed that Murrell was the leader of a gang with three hundred members. In *Life on the Mississippi*, Mark Twain expanded this number to one thousand. Twain also said that one of Murrell's scams was taking the role of a circuit rider. While he was preaching in church, his gang members stole the congregation's horses. Stewart said that the gang's base of operations was the Mississippi River—the Devil's Punch Bowl in Natchez, Mississippi, and the Neutral Strip in Louisiana, primarily—because it was a breeding ground for outlaws in the first half of the nineteenth century. He was reputed to have used a cave dug into the hillside in Sabine Parish in the community of Clearwater as one of his hideouts. The ground above the cave is now pockmarked with holes dug by treasure hunters using well-drilling equipment. Murrell's largest hideout, known as Murrell's Cave, was actually an intricate network of caves consisting of rooms where the gang supposedly deposited its ill-gotten gains, as well as its horses and mules. Carvings on trees and rocks gave directions to the caves. The caves were dynamited in 1942 by the U.S. Park Service to prevent people from getting lost or injured while exploring them.

A number of historians consider much of Stewart's book's content to be fiction. One of Stewart's most fanciful assertions was that Murrell and his gang had planned to take over New Orleans. This discredited claim, together with rumors that Murrell was going to lead a slave insurrection, led to a wave of paranoia known as the Murrell Excitement in much of the South. To this day, historians find the task of separating the myth from the man to be daunting, if not impossible.

5.
LOST TREASURE

I'SLE DE GOMBI

Gombi Island

Although buried pirate treasure has been the stuff of legend for centuries, the only known pirate who actually did bury his treasure was Captain William Kidd. He buried some of his booty on Gardiners Island near Long Island. One of the earliest—and most famous—Captain Kidd legends begins in 1701, when a dying sailor said that he had been a member of Captain Kidd's pirate crew and that they had buried approximately £2 million on Oak Island, off the coast of Nova Scotia. In 1795, a teenager named Dennis McGinnis and three of his friends were fishing when they found a depression on the ground on Oak Island. After encountering several oak platforms every ten feet, the young men gave up their search. Since then, a number of attempts have been made to find the treasure. The fact that nothing more than a few buttons, coins, pieces of jewelry, iron artifacts and hand-hewn pieces of wood have been found has not deterred people from sinking millions of dollars—and holes—into the dig sites on Oak Island. This deep-set urge to uncover buried treasure is the basis for the legend of the pirate treasure of Gombi Island.

Lyle Saxon recounts the legend of Gombi Island in his book *Gumbo Ya-Ya*. Years ago, a young man remembered only as Louis decided to dig for pirate treasure at L'Isle de Gombi near the mouth of Bayou Caillou. He beached his boat on the small island and proceeded to dig. Suddenly, he looked behind him and was alarmed to see his pirogue floating away, even though he had dragged it a good distance up on the beach. He jumped in the water and retrieved his boat. This time, he tied it to a small tree. He returned to the hole and resumed digging. Suddenly, something compelled him to look up. Standing over him were three pirates. Each of them held a bloodstained knife. Being a devout Catholic, Louis fell to his knees and promised the Virgin Mary that he would stop searching for treasure if she saved him from the pirates. When he opened his eyes, Louis observed that sea water was dripping from their clothes, and shrimp clung to their hair and beards.

Louis jumped up and ran to the pirogue, leaving his shovel and all thoughts of buried treasure behind him. As soon as he climbed into the little boat, the captain of the pirates materialized in the seat next to him. Louis recalled that blood dripped from his beard and shrimp crawled all over his face. In one hand, the pirate was holding a pistol. In a deep, guttural voice, the ghost of the pirate growled, "Row!" After Louis had rowed a good distance from L'Isle de Gombi, the ghost of the pirate slid off the pirogue into the Gulf.

Louis made it home in record time. When he walked through the front door, his wife took one look at him and started beating him on the head. When she realized that he really was her husband, she told him that she had attacked him because she did not recognize him. His hair had turned completely white.

The King of Honey Island Swamp

Slidell

In the late eighteenth and early nineteenth centuries, Honey Island Swamp was a well-known hideout for pirates and outlaws. With Bataria Bay on one side and Honey Island Swamp on the other, New Orleans was hedged in by pirates. The territory west of the Mississippi was the hunting ground of Jean Lafitte. A pirate named Pierre Rameau operated eastward, along the Bay of St. Louis, Pearl River and Honey Island Swamp. The amount of piracy in the region proliferated along the coast until General Andrew Jackson took control of New Orleans. Rameau was the ringleader of one of these gangs of cutthroats called the Chats Huats ("Screech Owls"). Born and raised in Scotland, the "King of Honey Island Swamp," as he became known, procured much of his booty from Alabama, Mississippi, Tennessee and North and South Carolina. Rameau often went under the name of Colonel Loring in New Orleans. Unlike Lafitte, who was satisfied with being a pirate, Rameau aspired to be accepted in high society as a gentleman. He claimed to have made a fortune as the owner of an immensely profitable mine, although some of the people in his social circle realized that his wealth really came from robberies, some of which involved murder. In Waveland, Mississippi, for example, Rameau robbed a rich man of his precious gems, tied him up and set his house afire.

Despite his "secret life" as a pirate, Rameau's rich and powerful friends tried to use their influence to secure him a place on Andrew Jackson's staff in New Orleans. Jackson denied their request, claiming that he already had enough staff officers, so Rameau retaliated by offering his services to Jackson's opponent, the British general. Major General Sir Edward Pakenham was pleased with the maps and drawings of Jackson's line that Rameau offered him. Rameau was severely wounded in both arms while fighting on the side of the British during the Battle of New Orleans and

The treasure of a pirate named Pierre Rameau is said to be buried in Honey Island Swamp, which he and other outlaws used as a hideout. *Wikimedia Commons.*

sought refuge at the home of a Creole friend. While the ladies of the house tended to his wounds, a personal enemy of his named Vasseur barged into the room and sprang at him with a dagger, screaming, "Die, Pierre Rameau, die, die!" Rameau kicked him so hard that he crushed Vasseur's chest. Ramaeau left the house and staggered into the woods, where he eventually got lost and died. Some of Rameau's friends found his body and buried him under a spreading oak tree.

Unlike some of Louisiana's pirates whose treasure is still waiting to be found, a cache of Pierre Rameau's pirate booty was discovered in Honey Island Swamp. The November 23, 1907 edition of the *New Orleans Item* newspaper reported that two hunters, Monroe Tally and James Culbert, dug up $1,000 in Mexican gold coins. Most of the coins were dated 1827. Miraculously, they were in good condition. Nothing else of value was found at the site. Because a number of desperados hid out around the Pearl River and Honey Island Swamp area, chances are good that more treasure will be discovered some day.

THE MISSING TREASURE CHESTS
OF PARLANGE PLANTATION

Pointe Coupee Parish

Vincent de Ternant founded an indigo plantation on ten thousand acres that he received from a French land grant. In 1750, he built the Parlange plantation house in the French colonial style. The two-story cottage is set on a raised-brick basement. The veranda is supported with brick pillars. Enslaved people made the bricks used in the construction of the house. The plaster used in the interior and exterior walls was made of mud, sand, animal hair and Spanish moss. Cypress planks were used in the walls and ceilings.

Vincent de Termant's son, Claude, inherited the plantation house and the plantation itself. Under his management, the plantation's cash crops shifted from indigo to cotton and sugarcane. His wife, Virginie, embellished the house with fine furnishings, including a number of family portraits, and after Claude died, Virginie married Charles Parlange, a colonel in the French army. She and her second husband divided much of their time between New Orleans and Paris. By the time war was declared in 1861, Virginie, who was widowed again, was living in Paris. As the Union army, under the command

A chest of gold and silver coins, which was hidden by the owner of Parlange plantation to keep it from the encroaching Union army, has still not been found. *Wikimedia Commons.*

of Nathaniel Banks, approached the plantation, she returned to Parlange and immediately set about protecting her valuables from the encroaching Union army. With the help of two trusted servants and her son, Charles, Virginie filled two wooden chests with silver, china, portraits and clothing. The third chest contained approximately $400,000 in gold and silver coins. She then buried the chests before the troops approached. General Nathaniel Banks and his troops arrived at Parlange plantation, and Virginie charmed him by treating him and his staff to a lavish banquet and allowing them to sleep inside the mansion. He reciprocated her kindness by sparing the house and the plantation from destruction.

Like many Southern aristocrats, Virginie's fortunes declined after the Civil War, so much so that she was reduced to making her own clothes. In 1867, Virginie's widowed daughter, Marie Virginie Avegno, moved to Paris with her only child, Virginie Amelie Avegno. Over time, Virginie Avegno married well and became a Paris socialite. Virginie achieved notoriety as the subject of Joseph Sargent's painting *Madame X*. Charles and Virginie's son, Charles, became one of Louisiana's most noted statesmen, serving as a state senator, United States district attorney, lieutenant governor, federal judge and justice of the Louisiana Supreme Court.

After Virginie Parlange died in 1887, Parlange plantation stood vacant for twenty years. In 1907, her grandson Walter Parlange moved into the house and took up the life of a farmer. As of 2020, Walter's descendants were still living at Parlange plantation. Today, Parlange plantation is open for tours. Aside from the home's beauty and historic value, some people are drawn to Parlange plantation because of the legend of buried treasure. It is said that in 1865, at the end of the war, Virginie dug up two of the chests, but the chest containing the gold and silver coins could not be found. All attempts to locate the coins have failed.

The Mystery of Norman Frisbee's Silver Bell

Tensas Parish

The story of Colonel Norman Frisbee bears a strong resemblance to that of the protagonist of William Faulkner's 1936 novel *Absalom, Absalom!*, Thomas Sutpen. Like Sutpen, Norman Frisbee was a dream-driven man who dared to venture into the wilderness and carve out a large plantation. In 1849, Frisbee began purchasing tracts of land in Tensas Parish, Louisiana, with the intention of becoming a cotton planter. In 1855, he and his wife, Anna, moved to Tensas from Claiborne County, Mississippi. Until 1860, Frisbee continued increasing the size of his plantation through sheriff's sales and from a number of individual landowners. He envisioned growing as much as ten thousand acres someday. Not much is known about Frisbee's house, which disappeared long ago. It was said to have had one-hundred-foot pillars set on a one-hundred-foot-square floor base. In 1912, older residents of Tensas Parish told Frisbee's granddaughter A.M. George that when Frisbee was told by a friend that the slave-made brick he was using in the construction of the house was inferior, he purchased new brick from New Orleans. The rafters of the house were made from cedar trees on his property. The beams were meticulously fitted together using the tongue-and-groove method. When the river proved to be too low for a steam packet to transport them down the Black River, he had a sawmill construct a specially made raft that would float its heavy cargo through relatively shallow water. Older residents of Tensas Parish recalled that the furnishings—iron railings, fine paintings, artists' busts, stained glass panes—were as fine as any found in New Orleans or Natchez.

Until the Civil War, Norman's prospects seemed promising. His wife, Anna, whom he married in 1843, bore seven children. However, by 1861, Norman had purchased so much land—approximately thirty-eight thousand acres—that he had fallen into debt, which was exacerbated by the cost of building his mansion and operating the plantation. He immediately ordered his slaves to build levees around his mansion to create a fortification against the invading Union army from deep in the Tensas Swamp. With a mound of debt looming over him, Norman became a desperate, quick-tempered man who drove his slaves mercilessly in the hope that a good cotton crop would save him. On November 24, 1864, Orlando Flowers, who had married Norman's sister Gertrude, was driving his stock past the Frisbee mansion on his way to join the Confederates in Texas. When one of Norman's mules joined Flowers's herd, Norman mounted his big bay horse and set out after his brother-in-law. He finally caught up with Flowers at a ferry landing on the bayou. Witnesses reported that Frisbee, still sitting astride his horse, lashed out Flowers, knocking him to the ground. In a rage, Norman jumped from his horse; Flowers rose up, and the two men began pummeling each other. Flowers pulled a knife and stabbed Norman to death. A faithful slave loaded him onto his horse and took him home. Anna was able to operate the plantation for a few years after his death, although she had to sell off pieces of land to pay her husband's debts. Sometime after 1870, a large number of lawsuits and demanding creditors forced Anna to sell the plantation.

By 1957, little remained of Frisbee's mansion, except for thirty-two pillars, some of which lay in pieces on the ground. The Old Brick House, as it came to be known, was nothing more than a large pile of bricks in the center of the columns where the roof fell in. In fact, Norman Frisbee himself would be completely forgotten were in not for the treasure story that keeps his memory alive. Between 1850 and 1860, Frisbee installed a silver bell on the top of his towering house. According to reporter Sam Hannah's 1957 article "Frisbee House," Norman probably had the bell transported to the mansion from Natchez. An older man recalled seeing the bell in the ruins of the mansion, although the swamp's thick undergrowth prevented him from getting a close look. The legend of the silver bell, as recounted by Beth B. Shelton, is much more romantic. In 1863, as General Grant's army was converging on Vicksburg, Norman Frisbee, like many planters at this time, was plagued with the fear that the Yankees would pillage his plantation. One day, Frisbee and two slaves loaded a wagon with one thousand pounds of silver coins and drove it to Natchez, where the coins were melted down to make a magnificent plantation bell. Frisbee had the bell painted with stain so that it would be overlooked by looters if the time came. After he returned to Tensas Parish and had the bell installed, Frisbee killed the two slaves to keep the secret of the bell safe. After Norman Frisbee was stabbed to death and his wife struggled to operate the plantation, a loyal slave persuaded Anna to allow him to bury the bell. He marked the spot with two spikes, half an inch in diameter, one on the south side facing north and the other on the east side facing west. The silver bell was buried at the intersection of the two spikes. For many years, hunters and trappers passed by the spikes, totally unaware of the significance. A band of gypsies searched for the bell but claimed that their efforts were thwarted by the spirit of Norman Frisbee.

The Lost Treasure of Charles Duralde

St. Martinsville

The devastating effects of the Civil War on the South cannot be overestimated. The changes wrought by the war were so dramatic, in fact, that the history of the South is marked by the antebellum and the Reconstruction periods. Legends that are still told in large and small southern towns recount strong southern women who saved their plantation homes through their charm and sheer defiance. Stories are also told of starving Union soldiers who stole everything that was not nailed down, including gold, silver, jewelry and food. Some planters who had nothing left to offer the invaders stood by helplessly while their mansion was burned to the ground. The possibility that the plantation owners buried their most prized possessions somewhere on the grounds has attracted hundreds of treasure hunters to the sites of old plantations. Such a legend is the story of Charles Duralde.

Lyle Saxon narrates the saga of Charles Duralde in his book *Gumbo Ya-Ya*. Duralde settled on ten thousand acres near St. Martinsville in the early 1800s. Hundreds of slaves worked the plantation. Duralde, who married twice, is said to have fathered twelve children from each of his wives. Many of the specifics of Duralde's life have been lost to time. However, people still talk about the double wedding of two of Duralde's daughters, who married into some of Louisiana's finest families. Duralde was determined to make the wedding the social event of the season in St. Martinsville. Several weeks before the wedding, Duralde ordered a cargo of spiders, which he set loose among the grove of pine trees on the grounds. After the spiders spun webs among the branches, Duralde's slaves sprinkled them with gold and silver dust to create a fairy-tale effect. On the day of the wedding, the procession paraded under the sparkling canopy of spider webs to the altar that had been set up in front of the mansion. Two thousand guests dined on fine food and wine during the reception.

It is said that the everyday lives of Duralde and his family were equally lavish. Every morning, slaves sprayed every room in the house with expensive cologne. Duralde and his family bathed in cologne, as well. The carriages that he and his family drove around St. Martinsville also reflected their prosperity. The outsides of the carriages were decorated with golden filigree. Inside the carriages, occupants sat on gold upholstery.

The Civil War brought an end to the patrician lifestyle of Charles Duralde and his family, just as it did for so many other wealthy planters in the Deep South. Devoted to the Southern cause, Duralde, his sons and his grandsons all fought on the side of the Confederacy. When Duralde returned home in 1865, he was shocked to find the entire plantation in ruins. His slaves were nowhere to be found. Before Duralde died a few years after the war, he hinted to his family members that he had protected his gold and silver from the hands of the Yankees. Sometimes, he said that he buried it on the grounds; at other times, he said that he had deposited it in a foreign bank. He died before he could reveal the exact location of his fortune.

JEAN LAFITTE'S TREASURE

South Louisiana Coast

Jean Lafitte (1780–1823) is one of the most colorful figures in the history of Louisiana. The first twenty years of his life are shrouded in mystery. Lafitte believed that he was born either in Saint-Domingue or in the French Basque Country. His biographer, William C. Davis, says that Lafitte was born near Pauillac, France, and that he sailed on ships owned by his father, a trader. The violence of the Haitian revolution drove him to board a refugee ship for New Orleans. By 1806, Jean Lafitte and his older brother, Pierre, had a smuggling operation in New Orleans. By 1808, Jean Lafitte became known as the "King of Barataria Bay," where he outfitted privateers and smuggled stolen goods. After the United States district attorney John R. Grymes charged Lafitte with violating the revenue law, forty soldiers descended on Barataria on September 13, 1814, capturing Lafitte and Pierre, as well as twenty-five smugglers. Lafitte and his men posted bond but refused to return for trial. On September 13, 1814, Commodore Daniel Patterson's fleet of six gunboats captured eight of Lafitte's ships, but Lafitte escaped.

Lafitte's road to vindication began on December 1, 1814, when Andrew Jackson arrived in New Orleans, only to find that the city's defenses were totally inadequate for the challenge presented by the oncoming British troops. Although the city had Lafitte's eight ships, there were not enough sailors to man them. Most of the city's one thousand troops were untested in battle. Two weeks after Jackson's arrival, Lafitte agreed to join the U.S. forces against the British if he and his men were granted a full pardon. After the state legislature passed a resolution granting the pardon, many of Lafitte's men manned the ships or joined the militia. When the British fleet sailed down the Mississippi River, Jackson took Lafitte's advice and extended the city's line of defense to the swamp. With the help of Lafitte's pirate gunners, Lafitte's former ships repulsed the British attack. On January 21, 1815, Jackson praised Lafitte's men and requested clemency for them. Their full pardon was granted on February 6, 1815.

Between 1815 and 1816, Jean and Pierre served as spies for Spain in the Mexican War of Independence. While Pierre reported back to Spain on the situation in New Orleans, Jean went to Galveston, which the revolutionaries had made their base. After the revolutionaries left the island, Lafitte converted Galveston into a smuggling base. Over the next year, the size of the pirate colony, which Lafitte called "Campeche," included one to two hundred men. By the end of the decade, the size of the colony had grown to approximately two thousand men, and its annual income, based on stolen goods and slaves, exceeded $2 million. Lafitte was forced to leave Galveston by the schooner USS *Enterprise* in 1821. It was said that he took large amounts of gold and treasure with him. For the next two years, Lafitte's pirate crew plundered Spanish ships off the Gulf of Mexico. According to one account, Lafitte died on February 5, 1823, while trying to take two heavily armed Spanish merchant vessels off the town of Omoa, Honduras. According to another account, Lafitte died of fever on the island of Mugeres, off the coast of Yucatan, in 1826.

Lafitte's treasury is said to have been buried in many places along coastal Louisiana. However, the best locales for a serious search of Lafitte's treasure are believed to be Grand Isle, where Lafitte made his headquarters; Coca

Pirate Jean Lafitte will always be remembered for the role he played in General Andrew Jackson's victory at the Battle of New Orleans. *Wikimedia Commons*.

Island, where Lafitte and his men often landed; and Kelso's Island, where a cache of $1 million in gold is said to be buried. In an article published in *Modern Mechanix* in March 1956, titled "Looking for Louisiana's Lost Loot," William L. Rivers tells the story of a writer named Ben Luien Burman, who went to the south Louisiana swamps to write a fur trapping story and encountered two men who were rumored to have found one of Lafitte's caches of gold. Although the men never admitted it, their friends and neighbors guessed that they probably had stumbled on the gold because, in the words of one of the locals, they "ain't done a lick of work in their lives. Everybody knows it's because they found where Lafitte's money was buried."

Many of these tales of Lafitte's buried treasure are probably apocryphal. However, some of Lafitte's treasure might have already been found. In his book *Gumbo Ya-Ya*, author Lyle Saxon wrote about a treasure hunter from New Orleans named John Patorno, who invented a radio device with an affinity for nonmagnetic metals. In 1935, Patorno and a ferry boat captain from Algiers named Clarke went to Coca Island with a map showing the location of Lafitte's gold. According to legend, two of Lafitte's pirates transported several chests of silver to Coca Island. After burying the chests, the men got into a drunken brawl. One of them died on the spot. The other pirate was mortally wounded, but a local fisherman nursed him back to health. The pirate showed his gratitude by giving him the treasure map, which Patorno and the ferry pilot took to Cealmost. They were almost buried alive in mud when the side of the pit they were digging caved in. Frustrated, the men reluctantly decided that forfeiting their lives was too high of a price to pay for buried treasure. Still, Patorno never lost the burning desire to find Lafitte's gold. A short while later, he found $1,300 in two caskets just across the Mississippi River from New Orleans.

JOHN FLETCHER'S BURIED TREASURE

Jasper County

Between 1800 and 1820, mule trains of gold and silver made their way from San Antonio, Texas, and Nuevo Laredo and Piedras Negras, Mexico, through the Neutral Strip of Louisiana. They usually stopped at Natchitoches to make hardware purchases, which the occupants paid for in gold bullion. These pack trains were easy prey for robbers in Jasper and Newton Counties. In 1816, the gold from one of these mule trains was buried somewhere in Jasper County for safekeeping. The story behind the gold was written in a letter by John Fletcher in 1816. Fletcher wrote that on April 7, 1813, he and twelve other men captured twelve mule loads of silver on Nolan's Trail from Natchitoches on Red River to San Antonio. On October 26, 1813, the men captured thirty mule loads of Spanish gold, as well as five other small lots. Fletcher and his comrades transported the gold to a small creek fifteen or twenty miles west of the Sabine River and put it under a waterfall. Because they did not mark the site, the exact location of the treasure was secreted away in the minds of Fletcher and his men. On the way back home, they were attacked by Andrew Jackson's cavalry. Nine of Fletcher's men died in the melee. Fletcher and two others were thrown in prison. One of Fletcher's friends died shortly after being imprisoned. Fletcher and his surviving partner were told that they could spend the rest of their lives in prison or fight the British in New Orleans. Fletcher and his friend chose the latter course of action. During the Battle of New Orleans, Fletcher's friend was killed, leaving Fletcher as the only person who knew the location of the treasure.

Fletcher's letter, along with a crude hand-drawn map, was passed down through the family of W.S. Glenn of Palestine, Texas. Glenn's ancestors moved to what is now Jasper County before the Texas Revolution. Glenn determined from the letter that Fletcher's gold was buried on a creek on his parents' farm in Jasper County, even though the waterfall mentioned in the letter was no longer there. In 1898, Glenn and several of his friends and family members founded the Palestine Prospecting Company. They raised $5,000 in operating expenses through the sale of one hundred shares of stock. One-fourteenth of the treasure would be designated as a royalty for W.S. Glenn. In the summer of 1898, Glenn used some the best treasure-hunting devices of the day to pinpoint the location of the treasure-trove. He hired a gang of laborers to dig on a high ridge on the east bank of the creek. By October of that year, Glenn had spent all of the investors' money without discovering the gold and treasure. Tired and frustrated, Glenn called off the search.

Interestingly enough, no one has tried to find Fletcher's gold since W.S. Glenn's failed attempt. The primary reason lies in the fact that there is no record in the county clerk's office of a deed to W.S. Glenn in the 1890s. The possibility exists that Glenn was excavating along the wrong creek and that the gold is still hidden along one of the many streams and creeks in Jasper County.

FORT DE LA BOULAYE

Natchitoches

In 1698, King Louis IV dispatched soldiers, Jesuit priests and cartographers to occupy the Louisiana Territory. Along with supplies and weapons, the group brought along $160,000 in gold and silver coins to expedite trade and to pay the members of the expeditions. Knowing that the British also had designs on the region, Louis ordered that a series of forts be built along the Mississippi River. An expedition led by Pierre le Moyne d'Iberville and his brothers, Jean-Baptiste Le Moyne de Bienville and Antoine Le Moyne de Chateauguay, was assigned the task of rediscovering the mouth of the Mississippi River. In 1698, d'Iberville left France with four ships and seventy men. After establishing a temporary settlement near what is now Biloxi, Mississippi, d'Iberville led three ships to the mouth of the Mississippi River.

Pierre LeMoyne d'Iberville supervised the construction of Fort de la Boulaye in 1700. *Wikimedia Commons.*

Finding nothing but swamp land, d'Iberville returned to Biloxi. Several months later, d'Iberville's expedition found a spot fifty miles upriver on high ground, where a fort could block British forces from sailing up the Mississippi. Construction of Fort du Mississippi began in 1699. D'Iberville's men cut down dozens of cypress trees and floated them to the building site. By 1700, the main buildings and magazine were completed. The fort was renamed Fort de la Boulaye, after a small village in eastern France. It was a wooden stockade with a two-story twenty-eight-foot-square log blockhouse. The fort was defended with six cannon and eighteen soldiers. British ships that made it as far as the fort were told to turn around. To this day, this place on the river is known as the English Turn.

The location of the fort was far from ideal. The area was flooded by frequent storms and hurricanes. The flooding problem was aggravated by strong winds that blew the waters onto the land and destroyed the colonists' flimsy shelters. Fort de la Boulaye was finally abandoned in 1707, when increasing pressure from the hostile Caddoan Indian tribe forced the French to evacuate the fort and move to Biloxi. The colonists took the bare necessities on the long trip to Biloxi, leaving behind many personal items. D'Iberville decided that the $160,000 in gold and silver coins was too heavy to carry over the swampy bottomlands, so he ordered the money to be placed in two wooden chests and buried. Some historians believe that the cache of coins was buried in a garden; others insist that the chests were probably interred in the dirt floor of the fort. A member of the expedition who had made friends with the Caddo people remained at the fort, which he converted into a trading post. During this time, a number of French troops were garrisoned at the fort. When St. Dennis was assigned to defend the western boundaries of New France, Fort de la Boulaye was abandoned.

The French had planned to return to Fort de la Boulay some day and retrieve the two chests of coins, but they were prevented from doing so by the eroding relations with Native tribes and the frequency of hurricanes. Over time, storms and floods destroyed great portions of the port. Eventually, nature reclaimed the area, hiding it from sight with brambles, trees and creeping vines. The fort was isolated even more after flooding forced the Mississippi River to change its course in the mid-eighteenth century. Remnants of Fort de la Boulaye were discovered in 1923, when Senator Joseph Gravolet began dredging a canal on his property to drain the nearby swamp. He was astonished when workers discovered ninety-two hand-hewn cypress timbers, most of which bore evidence of having been burned. In 1936, a cannonball was discovered. Since then, archaeologists have discovered the fort's exact location, finding remnants of a palisade. Fort de la Boulaye has been designated a national historic landmark. A historical marker has been erected at the site, but it is difficult to find.

Treasure hunters have been searching for the buried chests of coins for many years. Some people believe the treasure is so elusive because the weight of the chests caused them to sink even farther in the ground. Hope that the gold can indeed be found was provided by two Tulane students in the mid-twentieth century. Using a mine detector at the site of the fort, they claimed to have found tantalizing evidence that the gold is still there.

6

MYSTERIES FROM THE SKIES

THE OTHER WORLDLY VISITOR

Gonzales

According to reports collected by the Mutual UFO Network (MUFON), some individuals appear to have been targeted by extraterrestrial beings. Some of these people are victims of alien abduction, such as Barney and Betty Hill, who were abducted in on September 19–20, 1961, while driving outside of Lancaster, New Hampshire, and Charlie Hickson and Calvin Parker, who were abducted from a pier on October 11, 1973, in Pascagoula, Mississippi. Rarely do aliens make house calls. This was the claim of Amber Flake, who said that in 1989, a UFO hovered over the roof of her home in Gonzales, Louisiana. She described it as being a dark metallic color with several lights emanating from inside the craft. One of her sisters was also a witness to the UFO. Flake said that the next day, men in suits knocked on the door and asked for permission to conduct an investigation. Suspecting that something was not right, Amber's mother, Donna McKinley, told them, "No" and shut the door.

This was not McKinley's only close encounter. Apparently, she had several experiences with UFOs, including an abduction. "I was walking, and then I don't remember anything. And then the next thing I knew, I was walking back to the house. When I went inside the house, they told me I had been gone for hours, and they were getting worried and were getting ready to go

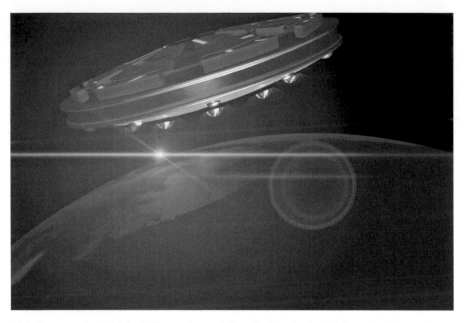

This likeness of a UFO is similar to the craft described by Amber Flake, who claimed that it hovered over her home in Gonzales in 1989. *Public domain.*

look for me." Afterward, McKinley created a number of airbrush paintings depicting the aliens.

Reginald Buck, the former state direct of Louisiana's chapter of MUFON, said that the military tends to dismiss reports like Flake's and McKinley's because "they don't want to spend that much money and that much time investigating something that they probably believe to be real but doesn't seem like a threat." Ironically, according to an article in the *New York Times*, the Pentagon budgeted $22 million on UFO research in 2017. The wave of UFO sightings in Louisiana is over, but other waves continue to this day.

THE JANUARY 1977 SIGHTINGS

Southeast Louisiana

Occasionally, UFO sightings appear in clusters over a short period of time. This was the case in January and February 1977, in Louisiana. On January 15, Peter Digangi and his wife were driving along Judge Perez Highway when, suddenly, bright lights appeared over a nearby water tower. They described the craft as "three lights chained together." The UFO hovered over the water tower for fifteen minutes before vanishing.

Less than a week later, on January 21, a couple of nutria hunters named Irwin Menesses and Robert Melerine were cruising through the bayou near the Yscloskey Shell refinery, when their otherwise routine hunt was interrupted by a very large light moving downward from the night sky. The craft's slow descent halted about seventy feet above the boat. At the same time, the boat stopped moving, even though the motor was still running. The astonished hunters were able to talk to each other, but their bodies seemed to be temporarily paralyzed. Afterward, they compared the sensation to being in suspended animation. Without warning, the UFO disappeared. Simultaneously, the invisible force that was controlling the men and the boat released its hold, and the boat shot ahead with such force that the men, who were standing up at the time, were jarred to the bottom of the boat. Before the men stood up, they glanced upward and noticed that the UFO was moving slowly around the oil refinery, almost as if the occupants were taking notes. The spacecraft remained visible for about thirty minutes.

The next day, Mark Bordeaux was standing on his front porch with his brother, Damian, taking in the night air, when a group of "reddish-orange lights suddenly appeared over the western side of New Orleans." Damien, who had worked at the local airport, could tell that the aircraft was not an airplane because the craft was larger and "did things airplanes cannot do." Not long thereafter, just outside of Chalmette, a car containing three adults and two children was heading toward the Jean Lafitte Parkway, when a dome-shaped aircraft of some sort descended in front of them. Looking outside of the left-side windows, the car's occupants observed several red and yellow lights moving around erratically in the sky. After about ten minutes, the dome-shaped craft soared over the woods and disappeared. The family was reluctant to share their eerie experience with anyone else, until they discovered that other people had seen it as well.

On January 25, Claire Wetta observed a cigar-shaped spaceship near the I-10 expressway. She described it as being "longer and narrower than the Goodyear Blimp." She also noticed a strange greenish glow coming from inside the spacecraft. Fifteen seconds after it appeared, the UFO disappeared.

The last of this series of sightings took place on February 8. Gayle Rodiguez and her son Brian were driving on the St. Bernard Highway, when the boy saw some sort of aircraft flying in the same direction as the car. He described the UFO as resembling a silver saucer with a domed top. Lights could be seen inside the dome and along the edge of the UFO. It was visible for only a few seconds before flying away.

Whatever was sighted in Louisiana made its way to Madison County, Mississippi, the next day in the little town of Flora. Deputy Sheriff Ken Creel and Deputy James Luke were headed toward Flora to check out a UFO report, when a UFO suddenly appeared. Hovering fifty feet above the patrol car, the craft emitted a strange light that disabled the car's radio. Several other people saw the craft.

THE MARKSVILLE FISH FALL

Marksville

Among the varied types of weather phenomena that have been reported over time, none is stranger—or more unsettling—than the weird things that have "rained" from the sky. Falls, as they have come to be known, first achieved national attention with the publication of Charles Fort's book *Book of the Damned* (1919). Fort spent years combing newspapers for accounts of strange natural phenomena, such as falls of fish and animals. Some of these strange occurrences were first reported in scholarly publications. For example, the *Scientific American* covered a large fish fall in Kansas City in 1873.

Louisiana's most famous fish fall took place in the little town of Marksville on October 23, 1947. A biologist with the Louisiana Department of Wildlife, A.D. Bajkov, was eating breakfast in a local restaurant when a waitress walked over to inform him that fish were falling from the sky. Spurred on by scientific curiosity, Bajkov dropped his fork and hurried outside. What he saw was a jaw-dropping spectacle. "There were spots on Main Street, in the vicinity of the bank (a half block from the restaurant) averaging one fish per square yard. Automobiles and trucks were running over them. Fish also fell on the roofs of houses....I personally collected from Main Street and several yards on Monroe Street a large jar of perfect specimens and preserved them in Formalin, in order to distribute them among several museums."

Italian scientist Raphael Eglini theorized in 1771 that heavy winds pick up small creatures like frogs and fish and deposited them miles away. Greg Carbin, a weather expert with the National Weather Service, agrees: "It is certainly within the realm of possibility that fish and frogs could rain from the sky. Especially when you look at the power of some thunderstorms and tornados, there's a tremendous vertical component to the wind that can suck things up and deposit them far from where they were picked up." The fact that most of these falls have been accompanied by heavy thunderstorms sand strong winds seems to support this theory. However, the Marksville fish fall is different in that no severe weather of any sort was reported in the area.

In 1961, Lola T. Dees noted in a report she filed with the U.S. Department of the Interior that winds did not exceed eight miles per hour in Marksville on October 23, 1947. "There was no tornado or updraft near Marksville," she wrote, "but there had been numerous small tornadoes the day before."

THE CASE OF THE BOOMING UFO

Kenner

Unexplained booming sounds have been reported all over the world. In the 1930s, French explorers in Greenland heard what they called deep, foghorn-like noise near Scoresby Sound. In Belgium, these thunderous sounds are called "fog belches." In the Bay of Bengal, people have been awakened by the "Bensal Guns." In America, these strange booms even received the literary treatment in Washington Irving's "Rip Van Winkle" and James Fenimore Cooper's "The Lake Gun." Explanations have ranged from fireworks displays to meteor showers. One of the most popular theories holds that these sounds are made either by experiment craft or by spaceships when they break the sound barrier. Indeed, some ufologists believe that extraterrestrials might have been responsible for a booming sound that was reported to MUFON in 2016 in Kenner, Louisiana.

Case 81061 from the MUFON witness reporting database was submitted by an unidentified resident of Kenner. On December 20, 2016, he walked out of his at house at 4:53 a.m. to try to find the source of "loud, booming-type base sound." Standing in front of his house, he saw a triangle-shaped UFO in the northern sky. He could tell that it was headed west. The witness described the craft as having three white lights in the shape of a triangle. Strangely, it emitted no sounds at all. Because the witness lived close to the airport, he knew what airplanes looked and sounded like. This aircraft, clearly, was no airplane. Included with the report was video footage that he took of the strange air ship. He added that he had seen a triangle-shaped craft once before, on March 2, 2007. This sighting took place ten miles from his house.

7

MYSTERIOUS CHARACTERS

THE PHANTOM WHISTLER

Paradis

The September 20, 1950 edition of the *Madera Tribune* published what was undoubtedly one of the strangest stories of the year. In February of that year, an eighteen-year-old girl named Jacqueline Cadow was asleep in the home she shared with her mother in Paradis, Louisiana, when she was awakened by someone wolf whistling outside of her bedroom window. A few days later, someone broke into the house, but nothing was taken. She notified the sheriff of the whistling and the break-in, but nothing was done. The whistling continued, night after night, for several weeks.

The Phantom Whistler's pattern changed after Jacqueline's engagement to a twenty-six-year-old state trooper named Herbert Belsom was announced in the local newspaper. That night, the Phantom Whistler appeared once more in the shrubbery outside of Jacqueline's bedroom window, but this time, he whistled Frederic Chopin's "Funeral March, Opus 35." Before the whistling stopped, Jacqueline heard a spine-tingling moan. Her claims were not taken very seriously by the authorities, until one night, when her mother, her aunt and a *States-Item* reporter heard the whistling from inside her room while Jacqueline was at work. They rushed outside, but by the time they reached the window, the intruder was gone.

The state police and the sheriff's office investigated the scene, but once again, no concrete evidence was found.

When the strange story was published in the local newspaper, throngs of curiosity-seekers drove by her house, hoping to catch a glimpse of the Phantom Whistler, as he was now known. As a result of all of the unwanted publicity, Jacqueline suffered a nervous collapse. After recovering, Jacqueline went to her relatives' house to stay, hoping that the whistling would stop. She discovered, however, on her very first night in the house that her tormentor was not easily deterred. The nightly whistling and moaning continued, driving her to seek refuge at the home of her fiancé's parents. On her first night at their house, Jacqueline's mother received a disturbing telephone call, saying, "Tell Jackie I know she's at Herbert's house."

On October 1, 1950, the day of Jacqueline and Herbert's wedding, the whistling ended as abruptly as it started. Afterward, the sheriff of Paradis stated that the Phantom Whistler was probably nothing more than "a hoax and inside job." He added that he knew who the whistler was, but he was reluctant to reveal his identity because he did not want to embarrass anyone.

JULIA BROWN: VOODOO PRIESTESS

Manchac Swamp

American folklore contains many legends pertaining to witches' curses. For example, between 1697 and 1698, the citizens of Leonardtown, Maryland, blamed their failed crops and outbreaks of disease on a woman named Moll Dyer, who they believed cursed the town. They set her house afire, but she escaped and ran into the woods, where she froze to death, clinging to a large boulder. Her hand and knee prints are still visible on that boulder. In 1884, a reputed witch living in Yazoo City, Mississippi, was accused of luring fishermen into her shack and torturing them. One night, they chased her into a swamp, where she got caught in quicksand. Before the muck covered her head, she swore that she would return and burn Yazoo City to the ground. In 1904, a devastating fire consumed 324 buildings. Heavy chains were laid on her grave in Glenwood Cemetery to keep her underground. In Louisiana, a similar tale is told about the Voodoo Priestess of Manchac Swamp.

To all appearances, Manchac Swamp is very inhospitable place, infested with swarming insects, poisonous snakes and alligators. Adding to its menacing aura is the water itself, which is covered with a pea-green coating of duckweed in the summer. However, according to local lore, Manchac Swamp was home to a Black woman named Julia Brown at the turn of the twentieth century. Born in Louisiana around 1845, she and her husband, a laborer named Celestin Brown, were given a forty-acre homestead by the federal government in 1900. Because the nearby town of Frenier did not have a doctor, she was able to make a living recommending herbal remedies, curing diseases and delivering babies. People said that in the evening just before dusk, Julia sat on her porch with her guitar and sang songs, some of which she had written herself. Over time, the locals started taking her for granted, demanding that she tend to their needs instead of asking her for help. After a while, she delighted in tormenting those who came to see her, with her predictions that bad things would befall them. Even her songs were imbued with a sinister tone. In the early 1900s, she began singing, "One day, I gonna die, and I'm gonna take one of you with me."

On September 28, 1915, Julia Brown died, apparently of natural causes. Her funeral was held the next day at her home in Frenier. According to an

Manchac Swamp is said to have been the home of Voodoo Priestess Julie Brown around the turn of the twentieth century. *Public domain.*

article that appeared in the *Times-Picayune* on October 2, 1915, her body was placed in a casket, which was sealed in a wooden box. The wind, which had been building all day long, rose to a furious pitch around 4:00 p.m. The 125-mile-per-hour winds completely destroyed the railroad depot, killing the twenty-five people who had sought refuge there. Over three hundred people in Frenier and nearby Ruddock died in the hurricane. Scores of buildings were washed away in the storm, including miles of railroad tracks. Little remained of Frenier in the aftermath, except for a large mass grave. Julia Brown's body and wooden box were retrieved, but her casket was never found. To this day, locals say that skeletons of some of the victims of the hurricane still emerge from the ooze of the swamp.

MARIE LAVEAU:
THE VOODOO QUEEN OF NEW ORLEANS

New Orleans

Marie Laveau has always been enveloped in mystery, partially because some of the facts of her life are unknown. Her birth date, which was never officially recorded, is probably around 1801. Although Marie's birth mother, Marguerite Darcantrel, was the mistress of a wealthy mixed-race businessman named Charles Laveaux, Marie was raised by Marguerite's mother, Catherine. Her childhood passed without note. On August 4, 1819, Laveau married a free Black carpenter from Haiti name Jacques Paris. The couple lived on Dauphine Street. Although the standard biographies usually omit any mention of the couple's children, the baptismal records from St. Louis Cathedral indicate that her daughters, Marie Angelie Paris and Felicite Paris, were baptized in 1823 and 1824, respectively. Felicite, however, was seven at the time of her baptism, which would make her birth date 1817.

In 1826, Laveau's life took a dramatic turn when she entered a common law marriage with a wealthy White man from New Orleans named Louis Christophe Dumensnil de Glapion. When her grandmother's house on St. Ann Street was put up for auction following her death, Glapion bought it for Marie. Rumors persisted for years that she and Glapion had fifteen children, but the birth records from that time list seven children, one of whom came to be known as Marie II. Laveau does not appear to have taken another lover or husband following Glapion's death in 1839.

The final resting place of Voodoo Queen Marie Laveau is without a doubt the most popular tomb in St. Louis Cemetery No. 1. *Wikipedia.*

Living alone, Laveau was forced to find employment to support herself and her children. Legend has it that she became a popular hairdresser for many of the well-to-do ladies in the French Quarter. Supposedly, she acquired a reputation as a clairvoyant by imparting information she had gleaned from listening to the gossip she overheard from the wealthy women she worked for as a hairdresser. It was not unusual to see fine carriages parked outside of Laveau's house on St. Ann Street during much of the day. Her alleged powers were renowned throughout the city.

By the end of her life, Laveau had become known as the Voodoo Queen of New Orleans. Many believe that she studied the practice of Voodoo under Sanite Dede, Marie Saloppe and Dr. John. On Sunday nights, she was a fixture at the gatherings on Congo Square, where she sold bags of herbs called gris-gris bags and gave readings. Legend has it that she also participated in exuberant singing and dancing.

Laveau also gained a reputation for her good works. She was a devout Catholic, who attended Mass every week. She was said to be a charitable soul, who used her magic and spells to help people. She even served as a sort of Catholic missionary to prisoners inside the Cabildo, offering them instruction in the faith.

Marie Laveau died on June 15, 1881, in her little house on St. Ann Street. Some of her followers, who confused her with her lookalike daughter, Marie Angelie, believed that she would never grow old. She was entombed in St. Loui Cemetery No. 1 as the "Widow Paris." Her influence in New Orleans persists to the present. Her name appears everywhere, from books and shops to apartment buildings. She has also become part of popular culture. In the third season of the television series *American Horror Story*, she was played by actress Angela Bassett. Marie Laveau might be dead, but she shows no signs of going away anytime soon.

8

MYSTERIOUS DEATHS

THE AXEMAN

New Orleans

The origins of jazz, which is has been called "American's Classical Music," can be traced back to the Black community living in New Orleans in the late nineteenth and early twentieth centuries. Jazz clearly developed from blues and ragtime music. However, many residents of the Crescent City believed that it originated in the tribal chants and ritual dances performed by enslaved people in Congo Square and then spread to the city's brothels and saloons. Consequently, jazz acquired negative connotations, prompting an editorial in the *Times-Picayune* to label it a "menace to society" in 1918. To no one's surprise, jazz became associated with a grisly string of murders committed that same year.

In the dead of night on May 25, 1918, an Italian grocer, Joseph Maggia, and his wife, Catherine, were attacked in their beds. Alerted by Joseph's moaning, his brothers rushed to the scene of the crime. They were horrified by what they found. The assailant had cut their throats with a straight razor before bashing in their heads with the blunt end of an axe. Catherine died instantly; Joseph followed her death three days later.

The fear instilled in the citizens of New Orleans by the senseless murders resurfaced a few weeks later. On June 27, 1918, another grocer, Louis Besumer, was sleeping in the back of his store with his mistress, Harriet Lowe, when they too were assaulted. The attacker struck Besumer above the right temple with an axe and chopped Lowe above the left ear. Although both of them survived, Lowe's face was partially paralyzed. Lowe underwent surgery on August 5 to repair the damage but died two days later. Besumer was charged with her murder and imprisoned for nine months, largely on the basis of a statement his mistress had made to the police shortly before her death, accusing him of attacking her. Besumer was acquitted on May 1, 1919.

New Orleans had barely recovered from the second attack before another one took place on August 5. A pregnant twenty-eight-year old woman, Anna Schneider, was lying in bed around midnight, when a dark figure approached her bed and began hacking away at her with an axe. Despite the gashes in her face, she not only survived her wounds but even gave birth to a healthy baby girl two days later. A suspect was arrested shortly thereafter but was released for lack of evidence.

Then, on August 10, the unthinkable happened again. The victim was another Italian grocer, Joseph Ramano, who lived with his two nieces. Woken by the sound of a struggle coming from their uncle's bedroom, the nieces burst through the door just in time to see a man run away. Later, they described him as a large, dark-skinned man wearing a dark suit and hat. Ramano was lying in his bed, bleeding profusely from a blow to the head. Just an hour or so later, he had recovered enough that he was able to walk to the ambulance and climb inside. However, his injuries were worse than he and his nieces had originally thought. Ramano died from severe head trauma two days later. At this time, the unknown assailant had been given a name in the press: the Axeman.

By the end of the year, the Axeman's reign of terror seemed to have ended. The city's terror was resurrected on March 10, 1919. Iorlando Jordano was inside his grocery store when he heard bloodcurdling screams coming from the home of his neighbor, Charles Cortimiglia. As he rushed across the street, Jordano was shocked to see Rosie Cortmiglia standing just inside the door with blood streaming down her face from a head wound. The dazed woman was holding her two-year-old daughter, Mary, who was dead. Her husband, Charlie, was lying on the floor with a large laceration to the head. Both husband and wife were immediately transported to the charity hospital by ambulance. Charlie recovered quickly and was released two days later. Rosie's stay in the hospital was more prolonged because she was in a coma. She eventually recovered physically, but she was never the same again mentally.

Owing to the lack of an apparent motive and the killer's seeming hatred for a specific segment of society, many people saw a similarity between the Axeman's murders in New Orleans and Jack the Ripper's murders in London. Like the Ripper, the Axeman also used the local newspapers to spread his messages. On March 13, 1919, the *Times-Picayune* published a letter it had received from someone claiming to be the Axeman. The writer began with the announcement that he had several other targets in mind and that that he would never be caught. His contention that he could have murdered someone every night but did not hinted that he was not as horrible as some people said he was. The most startling revelation came at the end of the letter, when the Axeman promised that the next Tuesday, he would pass over any house in New Orleans that was playing jazz, his favorite type of music. To this day, residents of New Orleans say that at quarter after midnight on Lenten Tuesday in 1919, the boisterous strains of jazz music echoed through the streets and alleys of New Orleans. For many, this was a rare reprieve from terror that had gripped the city. Ironically, the most maligned type of music in New Orleans offered the populace a glimmer of hope.

The maniac's penchant for Italian grocers became front-page news once again on August 10, 1919. Steve Boca was terrified by the sudden appearance of a large, dark figure standing over his bed with axe in hand. The man hit Boca in the head several times, eventually knocking him unconscious. After regaining his senses, Boca staggered outside and passed out in front of his neighbor's house. The fact that he could walk away was mindboggling, considering the extent of his injuries: Boca's brain was exposed through a large crack in his skull. Boca had no memory of the attack.

A nineteen-year-old girl, Sarah Lawman, was the next victim of the axe-wielding murderer's wrath. On September 3, 1919, she was asleep in her locked and shuttered home, when she was brutally attacked. The neighbors who came to her house to check on her reported that she had a gaping wound in her head, and several of her teeth were missing. Like Boca, she could not remember anything about the attack. A bloodstained axe was later found in the lawn by the police.

The Axeman's killing spree came to a bloody end on October 27, 1919. Alerted by noises coming from her bedroom, Esther Pepitone rushed inside, just as two men were running away. Her dead husband, Mike, lay on the bed. Afterward, the coroner determined that he had been struck by an axe eighteen times.

By the third attack, the police had become aware that the city was being terrorized by a serial killer. With the exception of the last two attacks, the killer's modus operandi was the same: he entered the houses by removing a panel from the back door. Most of his victims were Italian business owners. Eyewitness accounts of the survivors described the Axeman as a working-class male in his thirties. The police deduced that the skill with which he was able to break into the homes of his victims indicated that he was probably a practiced burglar.

Despite the efforts on the part of the police to attribute the crime as to a specific individual, the Axeman was never found. Miriam C. Davis, the author of *The Axeman of New Orleans: The True Story*, wrote, "The Axeman then disappeared from history. The Italians of New Orleans didn't. They continued to prosper. Although as a result of the growth of supermarkets, the corner groceries eventually disappeared, they, like so many immigrants before them, joined mainstream American society while continuing to preserve their own ethnic identity."

The Mystery of the Jennings 8

Jennings

In 2014, HBO aired the first season of a series titled *True Detective*. Set in southwest Louisiana, the show was about the unsolved murders of sex workers. The show revived local and national interest in a series of unsolved murders that took place in Jennings, Louisiana, between 2005 and 2009. Even though the creator of *True Detective*, Nick Pizzolatto, insists that the show was not based on the Jennings homicides, the similarities for people familiar with the case are unmistakable.

The first of these murders was reported on May 20, 2005, when a fisherman discovered the body of twenty-eight-year-old Loretta Lewis Chaisson floating in the river. A month later, the body of another woman, Ernestine Marie Daniels Patterson, was found. Her throat had been cut. The murder of Kristen Gary Lopez, twenty-one, in March 2007, added a new dimension to the murders: she was a witness to the shooting of a drug dealer by the police in 2005. The corpses of the next two murdered women were discovered along the side of a road, Witnei Dubois, twenty-seven, in May 2007 and Laconia "Muggy" Brown, twenty-three, in May 2008. The body of Crystal Shay Benoit Zeno, twenty-four, was found in a small wooded area in September 2008. Two months later, the body of Kristen Gary Lopez's seventeen-year-old cousin, Brittney Gary, was discovered just off a highway. The body of the last victim, Necole Guillory, twenty-six, turned up near I-10, a well-known drug corridor, not long after she was reported missing. The victims of these seemingly senseless homicides soon became known in the media as the Jennings 8.

The similarities between the victims indicated that they might have been murdered by a serial killer. Aside from being from the same town, they all lived outside of the law as sex workers or drug users. A number of them had also served as informants against drug dealers during investigations. They were all poor, they all had criminal records and they all knew each other.

In 2011, author and reporter Ethan Brown traveled to Jennings to investigate the case, which he had first read about in the *New York Times* the year before. He was intrigued by the fact that the local police had uncovered few leads, despite the fact that Jennings is a small town. The sinister aura that was attached to the case deepened when a drug dealer Brown had just interviewed, David Deshotel, was shot and killed in his house the next day. When Brown visited the house, he was struck by the fact that the crime scene had not been secured and that people were taking items from the house. His curiosity aroused, Brown delved into police personnel files, building liens and thousands of legal documents in his search for the truth. What he discovered was unsettling. Rumors were circulating that several police officers had previously had sex with some of the women. The truck in which one of the victims' throat was slashed had been tampered with. Two people connected with the case who had alerted the authorities about problems with the case—a sergeant and a prison nurse—lost their jobs. One of the most shocking pieces of evidence Brown found was another link between the victims: most of them had witnessed other murders before being killed themselves.

The book that grew out of Brown's research, *Murder on the Bayou*, caused quite a stir throughout the state. Brown's most damning revelation exposed a connection between Congressman Charles Boustany and the Boudreaux Inn, where all of the victims had taken their customers and used drugs. The hotel, it turned out, was co-owned by a field representative of Boustany's, Martin P. Guillory. Brown's book also included statements from witnesses testifying that Boustany was a client of several of the women. Following the book's publication, Boustany's communication director and Boustany's wife denied Brown's accusations. Many people in Jennings were not pleased with the book. Jefferson Davis Parish sheriff Ivy Woods attacked Brown for "insinuating corruption in our sheriff's office." The editor of the local newspaper retaliated, as well, publishing several articles accusing Brown of careless reporting.

Even though Brown's book strongly suggests corruption took place at the highest level, he never accuses anyone of the murders. The case is still open, fueling even more speculation about the identity and motives of the killer or killers. As far as the loved ones of the Jennings 8 are concerned, the fact that justice still has not been served only amplifies the tragedy of the victims' lives.

THE STRANGE DEATHS OF ERIC AND PAM ELLENDER

Sulphur

In the early 1990s, Eric and Pam Ellender were living in Sulphur, Louisiana, not far from Pam's parents. In high school, Pam was on the cheerleading squad and voted Homecoming queen. Eric was a bright young man with a penchant for business. After Eric married Pam, he went to work for his father-in-law, Huey Littleton. Their peaceful life in Sulphur came to a violent end on February 11, 1991, when they were shot to death in their bed. Their infant daughter, who was sleeping in the same room, was unharmed. The Ellenders' car was gone. On February 12, 1991, police apprehended four men who were in the Ellenders' car. One of the men, eighteen-year-old Chris Prudhomme, confessed to the murders. He admitted that he had killed the couple with Eric's shotgun, which they had found in the house. Not only did Prudhomme show no remorse for the killings, but he even claimed to have enjoyed taking their lives. Seventeen days after his arrest, Prudhomme was found hanging in his jail cell. He died a few hours after he was cut down. Inside the cell, guards found a suicide note in which he repeated what he had told police shortly after his arrest—that he was solely responsible for the Ellenders' murder and that he enjoyed doing it. The police considered the case closed.

However, Huey Littleton was not convinced that Prudhomme had worked alone. He believed that a local satanic cult known as Satan's Kids Against the Establishment was involved somehow. Over the next several months, Littleton interviewed over one hundred witnesses. In one of these interviews, a girlfriend of one of the cult members told him that the morning after the murders, a meeting of the cult was held, during which Prudhomme was instructed to take the blame for the crime to protect another cult member who had been with him at the time. The girl told Littleton that the two men had taken LSD and broke into the house to rob the Ellenders, but things got "out of hand," and they ended up killing the couple. Another young woman, Nickie Alderson, told Littleton that shortly after the murders, she and the other members held a party at the Ellenders' house. Alderson said that while she was doing drugs with the other members, she was totally unaware that the bodies of the owners of the house were lying in their bed upstairs.

The new information did not convince the police that the case should be reopened, so Littleton continued his investigation. Later, he found another witness, Chip Richards, who told him that he saw video taken inside the Ellenders' house showing the couple being murdered and sexually molested. The case took another strange turn when another one of the four men in the car, Robert Adkins, admitted to a friend, Shawn Moody, that he, too, was there when the Ellenders were killed. He said that Prudhomme shot Pam when she woke up. The blast of the shotgun woke Eric, so Prudhomme shot him too.

Another witness added another wrinkle to the case. Pearl Fruge told Littleton that her cousin, Kim Manuel, had witnessed the murders. Littleton persuaded Fruge to record Manuel, with the girl's permission. Manuel was indicted on the basis of the tape, which Fruge played for the grand jury. Manuel was indicted on two charges of second-degree murder. However, her court-appointed attorney, John Laverne, told authorities that Fruge had scripted the recording and that Manuel was unjustly convicted. One year later, the charges against her were dropped.

As a result of the overturned verdict, Littleton lost all credibility with the police. However, on February 9, 1994, Robert Adkins was indicted for his part in the murders and sentenced to twenty-one years in prison. However, because Adkins had already served time on the stolen car charge, the judge reduced the sentence to five and a half years. Adkins's accomplices, Phillip LeDeoux and Kurt Reeese, were given short terms as accessories after the fact.

With the arrest and conviction of Adkins and the other two men, the state of Louisiana considered the case closed. Huey Littleton, however, refused to rest until everyone involved in the murder of his daughter and son-in-law were brought to justice. With his death on July 15, 2019, it is unlikely that the case will ever be opened again.

THE BIZARRE END OF ZACK BOWDEN AND ADDIE HALL

New Orleans

Born in Los Angeles in 1978, Zack Bowden moved to New Orleans in the 1990s. In May 2000, he enlisted in the U.S. Army. He was a military police officer in Kosovo and Iraq. He was also stationed at Abu Ghraib prison for a while. Bowden served with distinction, earning a presidential unit citation and a NATO medal. However, he received a general discharge instead of an honorable discharge. As a result, he was entitled to VA benefits but not GI Bill education benefits. Along with the bitterness he felt about the way he was discharged, Bowden was also plagued with bouts of depression. One incident that contributed to his post-traumatic stress disorder was the death of a girl he had befriended in Iraq, when her family's shop was bombed.

He returned to New Orleans and found work as a bartender at several bars. He met and fell in love with another bartender, Addie Hall. Prior to meeting Hall, Zack had been married and divorced and had two children. Like Zack, Hall was a troubled soul. She told her friends that she had been abused as a child, a scarring experience that led her to a series of abusive relationships when she grew up. She was also a heavy drinker, like Zack, who was known to drink rounds of Jameson Irish Whiskey and Miller High Life while talking about his military service.

According to a story published about Zack and Addie in the *New York Times*, they fell in love during and after Hurricane Katrina. They were part of a handful of residents who refused to leave New Orleans, preferring to take their chances with the hurricane instead. For days, the couple lived in a damaged house with no electricity, devoting most of their time to feeding stray cats and mixing cocktails for their friends. Their relationship was not problem-free, however. Their friends reported that after Katrina, Zack and Addie argued a lot, probably because of Zack's infidelity and their escalating cocaine usage. On October 4, 2006, Addie told her landlord that she was kicking her boyfriend out because he was cheating on her. He told her to return to the apartment and have a serious talk with Zack. The landlord was the last person to see her alive.

Zack and Addie's story came to a tragic—and grisly—end on October 17, 2006. That evening, Zack was in the Omni Hotel drinking alone. Around 8:30 p.m., he finished his last drink and walked over to an outside terrace. Security cameras showed Zack running to the edge several times before finally jumping off, landing on the roof of the parking garage. Investigators found a note in Zack's back pocket, instructing them to send a patrol to 826 North Rampart Street, where they would find "the dismembered corpse of my girlfriend in the oven, on the stove, and in the fridge along with full documentation on the both of us and a full-signed confession from myself." Inside the apartment, the police found a scene of horrors. A severely burned human head was in one of the two pots on the stove, and her hands were in the other pot. Inside the oven, the police found charred arms and legs in a roasting pan. Chopped-up carrots and potatoes were on the counter. The torso had been placed in a plastic bag inside the refrigerator. In his confession, Zack admitted to killing Addie on October 5. The next morning, he went to work as usual. After work, he dismembered Addie's corpse in a bathtub with a knife and a hacksaw. He said he cooked the body parts to make them easier to dispose of. Zack ended his confession by stating, "I scared myself not only by the action of calmly strangling the woman I've loved for one and a half years, but by my entire lack of remorse."

The murder-suicide has left a dark imprint on New Orleans. A few years after their tragic deaths, Mary "Voodoo Queen" Millan leased the Rampart Street building and gave tours to the couple's apartment. In 2017, the TLC show *Paranormal Lockdown* filmed an overnight investigation of the infamous apartment. During the night, investigators reported feeling a cool breeze in the room, despite the fact that the windows were shut. The sensationalist nature of the crime, as well as the mystery surrounding the murder and the dismemberment of the corpse, ensure that Zack and Addie's tale will be told for years to come in New Orleans.

THE MYSTERY OF THE ILLICIT LOVERS

LaPlace

LaPlace, Louisiana, was unique during the French colonial period in Louisiana because it was originally settled by immigrants from Germany. Later, the German residents of the German settlement known as Karlstein intermarried with French and Acadian settlers. The region became known as Bonnet Carre ("Square Bonnet") because the Mississippi River makes a right angle here, forming what appears to be an old-fashioned bonnet. In 1811, LaPlace became the nexus of a slave rebellion, the largest in U.S. history.

In the mid-twentieth century, LaPlace's colorful history was enhanced by a sensationalistic unsolved murder case.

In 1956, an attractive thirty-one-year-old divorced mother of three from Baton Rouge, Audrey Moate, was having an affair with a married man, forty-six-year-old Thomas Hotard. At the time, Moate was working as a buyer at Kaiser. The couple covered up their relationship by telling their families that they had to work on Saturday, the day when they had been meeting in secret for two years. Interestingly enough, Hotard was often seen in her presence, but she introduced him as a friend of hers. The true nature of their "friendship" came out on November 24, 1956. Tom and Audrey left LaPlace at 7:30 a.m. and drove to a secluded "lovers' lane" near Lake Pontchartrain. Their presence in the area was confirmed by a father and son who were hunting in the area. At 9:00 a.m., the father and son saw a man and a woman in the back seat of a blue four-door sedan parked just a few yards from the lake. Later, authorities identified the couple as Thomas Hotard and Audrey Moate. Three hours later, another hunter saw the same car; Hotard was clearly visible in the back seat. The hunter decided not to check it out and left. The next day, the father and son who had originally found the car returned to the scene. When they opened the door, they were shocked to find Hotard dead in the backseat. He had been shot in the back. Police determined that the killer had pressed a shotgun against the rear window and fired. Hotard's lover, Audrey Moate, was gone.

Using evidence found at the site, investigators were able to re-create the couple's last moments together. Scattered on the ground near the car were the contents of a woman's purse. Audrey's shoes were found on the floor of the car. The police were particularly intrigued by two sets of footprints found near the car. The prints of a barefoot woman led to the woods. The fact that they were widely spaced suggested that she was running. The tracks of a man's boots found five feet from the car indicated that the man and woman had struggled. One the ground was a set of keys that might have dropped accidentally. The footprints stopped at a road leading to the highway. Motorcycle tracks were found on the road. The keys discovered at the scene belonged to Moate's car, which was found at the café where Hotard picked her up on November 24.

The mystery deepened two weeks later, when someone identifying herself as Audrey Moate called up Moate's former mother-in-law. The urgent voice on the phone said that the caller needed help quickly. After the caller hung up, Moate's mother-in-law was convinced that she had been speaking to Audrey. Not long after the phone call, a waitress who worked at the café where the car was found told police that she had seen a woman with tangled hair in the restaurant who seemed to match Audrey's description.

Investigators originally named Audrey Moate as the prime suspect in the murder of Thomas Hotard. They believed that she had run off after killing her boyfriend, but evidence found at the scene rendered this scenario improbable. Police pursued several false leads in the 1980s but came no closer to solving the crime. On March 15, 1989, the case received national attention when it aired in an episode of the television series *Unsolved Mysteries*. In 2011, Audrey Moate's daughter, Dekki Moate, gave her DNA to authorities to see if it matched the DNA in female remains that had just been discovered, but the results were not made public. What is certain is that Audrey Moate was never seen again, and her fate is unknown. Tom Hotard's killer has never been apprehended either.

9.

MYSTERIOUS DISAPPEARANCES

Hazel Head's Vanishing Act

Bossier City

Unlike some people who seem to drop off the face of the earth for no apparent reason, Hazel Head's disappearance was probably intentional. Most of what is known about her can be found in her police profile. Born on December 10, 1949, she has blond hair and green eyes and is five feet, two inches tall. Her weight is estimated to be 120–150 pounds. She has a gap between her teeth and a scar near her right eye. Hazel Head's ten marriages were part of her modus operandi. She wandered around the country under a variety of names, in search of lonely older men to marry or become involved with. After spending all of the man's money in his bank account, she moved on, often hitchhiking. She found many of her marks at truck stops. When she was between husbands, Hazel made a living as a waitress. In 1991, a warrant was issued for her arrest in Nebraska for burning down her boyfriend's trailer.

According to an episode of the television series *Unsolved Mysteries*, Hazel Head took out a want ad in the personal section of a Louisiana newspaper. Using the alias "Deianna Ray," Hazel described herself as "honest and hardworking." Her ad was answered by a retired truck driver named Charles Baker. Following the death of his wife of eleven years, Baker came into a sizable settlement from the insurance company. His penchant for gambling in the riverboat casinos in Bossier City brought him into contact with Hazel Head in the summer of 1998. She moved in with Baker just a few days after meeting him. A few weeks later, Baker confessed to his daughter, Cindy Jefferson, that his relationship with his new girlfriend was being strained. Cindy became worried when her father did not answer any of her phone calls. She conveyed her concerns to her aunt, June Steinger, who lived near his house. When June and her husband arrived at Baker's house on September 2, 1998, they were surprised that the front door was open. Inside the house, they found Charles Baker in the kitchen, slumped over the bar. He had been shot in the head.

The authorities arrived shortly thereafter. The coroner determined that Baker had been dead for five days. Investigators found Baker's handgun on the table. Someone had wiped the gun clean of fingerprints. There was no sign of a struggle anywhere inside the house. The bedroom safe, which had contained $45,000, was empty. Baker's Lincoln Town Car and girlfriend were gone, as well. The police added to the Hazel's seven-year-old arson charge car theft, first-degree murder and unlawful fight to avoid prosecution. Hazel Heard was last seen at a truck stop near Wheat Ridge, Colorado, where she applied for a job as a waitress in December 1998.

WHERE IS A.J. BREAUX?

Houma

In 1991, Adam John "A.J." Breaux was working as a salesman at a clothing store in Houma, Louisiana, a job that he had held for thirty years. He was married and had three daughters, but his growing problem with alcohol contributed to his divorce. Following a DUI arrest in 1983, Breaux decided it was time to sober up. He immediately enrolled in Alcoholics Anonymous and remained sober for the next eight years, even becoming a secretary for the local AA group and joining an adult support group called the Easy Does It Club. On August 28, Breaux left the club. At 10:00 p.m., on his way home, he stopped at a local convenience store to buy a quart of milk. When he did not return home afterward, his daughter, who he was living with at the time, notified the police the next day.

The police located his locked car two days later in a park across the street from the club. Inside the car were his wallet, his personal checkbook, the checkbook for the AA chapter and a bank bag filled with $165 earmarked for the AA chapter. There were no signs of a struggle. Oddly, the gallon of milk and the car keys were missing. Though he had bought $10 worth of gas at the convenience store, the tank in his car was nearly empty.

For the next few weeks, several witnesses came forward, claiming to have seen A.J. Breaux on the night of his disappearance. A man who claimed to know Breaux told police that he saw him riding in a compact car with three men eight miles out of town. He was puzzled when he waved at Breaux, but Breaux did not wave back. An eyewitness account given by an acquaintance of Breaux's, Kenneth Pellegrin, seemed to lend credence to the previous man's story. He said that as he was driving along, he saw a disheveled-looking A.J. Breaux standing in a phone booth outside of a convenience store. Breaux was wearing a "lumber jack" shirt at the time. The witness noticed three men sitting in a compact car parked in front of the convenience store. A third witness, Christy Bourdreaux, told police that on September 28, a man whose face she recognized from Breaux's missing person posters parked a van in front of her house and asked her if she would like to buy a bag of frozen fish. He was unkempt and reeked of alcohol. When she was shown a mug shot of Breaux from his 1983 DUI arrest, she swore that this was the man who came to her house. A fourth witness told authorities that he saw three men force a fourth man into a red compact, but he could not swear that this was Breaux. The police received a handwritten note stating that Breaux shot himself while drunk and his body tumbled over Bayou bank near the dam. The note was later proved to be a hoax.

The missing person's case of A.J. Breaux aired on a 1992 episode of *Unsolved Mysteries*. Unfortunately, the show did not produce any useful leads. Years after his disappearance, his daughters revealed that he was a closeted homosexual. However, no link has been found between Breaux's sexual orientation and his disappearance. Breaux was declared legally dead in 1998.

WHAT HAPPENED TO BOBBY DUNBAR?

Opelousas

Most parents would agree that the worst tragedy that could befall a family is the loss of a child. The long-lasting residual effects of such a horrific event could explain why the mystery of little Bobby Dunbar still resonates with people today. Bobby Dunbar was born to Lessie and Percy Dunbar in April 1908. In August 1912, he and his family went on a fishing trip to Swayze Lake in St. Landry Parish. The vacation went smoothly until August 23, when Bobby was nowhere to be found. The police immediately began a statewide search for the boy. Eight months later, a handyman and piano tuner named William Cantwell was spotted driving around Mississippi with a little boy who resembled the Bobby. Cantwell said that the child was the son of Julia Anderson, who worked for his family. Cantwell added that she had given him custody of the boy. The police arrested Cantwell and notified the Dunbar family that they had a boy who might be their son. Newspaper accounts of the reunion with the Dunbars and their "son" in Mississippi were mixed. One paper reported that the boy ran to Lessie Dunbar, screaming, "Mother." According to a different newspaper, the boy did not seem to recognize his younger brother, Alonzo. Before returning to Opelousas, Lessie bathed the boy and determined by the moles and scars on his body that he was indeed her son.

Meanwhile, Judith Anderson arrived in Opelousas from North Carolina to try to prove Cantwell's story and regain custody of her son. At the police station, she viewed a line-up of five boys, one of whom was the boy in Cantwell's car. The boy whom the Dunbars claimed as their son showed

The fate of little Bobby Dunbar, who disappeared during a fishing trip, is still unknown. *Wikimedia Commons.*

no signs that he recognized Anderson as his mother. When asked if he was her son, Anderson was uncertain. The next day, Anderson bathed the boy and, like Lessie Dunbar, claimed to have recognized the marks on his body. However, because of her inability to positively identify the boy as her son the day before, the judge dismissed her case. She briefly returned to Mississippi to testify to Cantwell's innocence at his trial in Poplarville. Despite her tearful insistence that a mistake was being made, "Bobby," as he was now known, was returned to the Dunbar family.

Over the next few decades, the primary figures in the case went on with their lives. Judith Anderson had such a warm reception in Poplarville that she decided to remain there. She married and had seven children. After serving two months in prison, Cantwell hit the road once again when the prosecution refused to file for a second trial. Before his death in 1945, Cantwell maintained his innocence. Bobby Dunbar married, had a wife, children and grandchildren and died in 1966.

The mystery of Bobby Dunbar's true identity persisted well into the twenty-first century. In the early 2000s, Bobby Dunbar's granddaughter Margaret Dunbar Cutright began her own investigation into her grandfather's case, perusing old newspaper stories and evidence presented by Cantwell's defense attorneys. In 2004, a reporter for the Associated Press approached the Dunbar family about writing a follow-up story on Bobby Dunbar. He told them that they could receive closure if Bob Dunbar Jr. agreed to undergo a DNA test. He agreed, and his sample was compared to a DNA sample taken from his cousin, the son of Alonzo Dunbar. The family was dumbfounded by the results: Bobby Dunbar was, in fact, not a blood relative of the Dunbar family. His case remains unsolved.

10

MYSTERIOUS MONSTERS

THE CASKET GIRLS OF THE OLD URSULINE CONVENT

New Orleans

New Orleans has been associated with vampires since the eighteenth century. One of the oldest surviving buildings in New Orleans is the Ursuline convent. In 1727, fourteen Ursuline nuns arrived in New Orleans from Rouen, France, after a five-month voyage. The academy they established was the first boarding school in Louisiana. The nuns were charged by King Louis XV of France to educate the daughters of wealthy Catholic families. Circumstances compelled the nuns to expand their mission during the War of 1812, when they tended to wounded American and British soldiers. Over time, the Ursulines also set up the first school of music in New Orleans, an orphanage and one of the city's first hospitals. For a while, most of their patients were soldiers, although the nuns also treated enslaved people who had contracted diseases.

After the nuns moved to the Ursuline convent in the Ninth Ward in 1823, the French Quarter Ursuline Convent became the Archbishop's palace. At the turn of the century, the old Ursuline convent housed the offices of the archdiocese. Later in the twentieth century, it became the rectory for nearby St. Mary's Cathedral. The first Ursuline convent was a three-story structure built mostly of wood. Because of the humid climate in New Orleans, the

The "casket girls," who were sent by the Bishop of Quebec to become wives in the French colonies along the Gulf Coast, lived with the nuns at the Ursuline Convent for a while. *Alan Brown.*

exposed wood rotted fairly quickly. In 1851, a two-story convent built with brick and stucco was completed using elements of the older structure, such as the wooden staircase. The dormitory, infirmary and classrooms were located on the ground floor. The cells for the nuns, a library, a second infirmary and a storeroom were on the second floor. The six beds in the attic were for the orphans. Today, the old Ursuline convent serves as the Catholic cultural heritage center of the Archdiocese of New Orleans.

The legend of the old Ursuline convent's association with vampirism begins with the "Casket Girls." The *files a la cassette* were young women who traveled to New Orleans with their *cassettes*, which is French for "caskets." They were part of a consignment of virtuous young women who were contracted by the bishop of Quebec to several cities on the Gulf Coast to become wives of men in the French colonies. They arrived in New Orleans in 1728. The girls lived with the Ursuline nuns until they found husbands, most of whom were fur trappers.

Most of the legends swirling around the Casket Girls are derived from the mispronunciation of "Cassette Girls." In her book *New Orleans Vampires,* author Marita Woywod Crandle recounts a story that originated with Jean Baptiste le Moyne Bienville. In his tale, the girls' chaperone on the ship, Sister Gertrude, was jealous of the attention her charges received, so she arrived at an agreement with a vampire, who infected the girls with vampirism by taking the form of a cat, which could get much closer to them than he could. By the time the ship reached New Orleans, many of the passengers had died, victims of the maiden vampires. To Sister Gertrude's chagrin, the girls had become even more beautiful after they had "changed." The vampire maidens were kept in a house on Bienville Street until work on the convent was completed. In 1735, the nuns took the girls to the attic on the third floor of the convent, where they were fed the blood of dying patients in the infirmary. The shutters were nailed shut with nails blessed by the pope. To this day, many people walking by the old Ursuline convent on ghost tours have had the unsettling feeling that they were being watched by eyes peering through the gaps in the wooden shutters in the attic.

WHO WAS JACQUE ST. GERMAIN?

New Orleans

According to legend, a mysterious man who called himself Jacque St. Germain arrived in New Orleans. When he had found a place to live at 1039 Royal Street, St. Germain became a fixture in the city's social scene, largely because of his wealth and charm. He was very popular with the ladies, whom he entertained at his lavish dinner parties where his guests were served delicious food and fine wine. While they were eating, St. Germain regaled them with stories about ancient Italy, Africa and Egypt in such detail that he gave the impression of having lived in these places thousands of years ago. He also told his friends and acquaintances that he was a direct descendant of the Comte de St. Germain, a friend of King Louis XV around two hundred years earlier. People who had seen portraits of the Comte St. Germain were intrigued by the fact that he was painted when he was forty years old, the same age as Jacque St. Germain. The resemblance between the two men led some to conclude that they were the same man. If this were true, then Jacque St. Germain must have been immortal. His guests were struck by the fact that St. Germain never ate anything at his parties; he only drank what appeared to be wine from a chalice. Rumors spread soon after his arrival in New Orleans that he must be a vampire.

For many people, the truth regarding St. Germain's identity was revealed one night when a woman who was said to have been a prostitute jumped from his balcony. She told the people in the crowd that had formed around her that she leapt from the balcony after St. Germain had tried to bite her neck. She swore that he probably would have killed her had he not been interrupted by a knock on the door. While the woman was being taken to the hospital for treatment of her wounds, the police informed St. Germain that he could wait until the next morning to make a statement. They believed that the woman must have been delusional because a man of St. Germain's station would never have assaulted her.

To the surprise of the police department, St. Germain failed to show up at the station the next day. Later that morning, the police went to his house and knocked on the door. When St. Germain did not answer, the police broke in. Not only was St. Germain gone, but the second floor of his house contained corked bottles filled with a combination of wine and blood. The mysterious Jacque St. Germain had vanished without a trace. He was never seen again, in America or in Europe.

THE CURIOUS CASE OF THE CARTER BROTHERS

New Orleans

During the Great Depression, a series of murders enhanced New Orleans's growing reputation as a city where the supernatural was very much alive. In 1932, people walking down St. Ann Street were appalled by the sight of a bloody young woman staggering down the sidewalk as if in a daze. When the police took her to the hospital, they noticed that the girl's wrists had been slit. They deduced that she had not tried to commit suicide because the cuts were not deep enough. The young woman told them that two men had kidnapped her and drained the blood from her body. The authorities rushed to the address she had given them and knocked on the door. When no one answered, they barged in. They went upstairs and were horrified by the sight of fifteen bodies lying all over the room. All of the corpses had shallow cuts on their wrists. The police did not have to look very far for the occupants of the house, Wayne and John Carter. The officers attempted to arrest the brothers when they returned home from their job at the city docks. When Wayne and John walked through the door and saw the officers waiting for them, they jumped into action, knocking out four of them and jumping from the top floor balcony to the street below.

The police had no trouble apprehending the "vampire brothers" because they were creatures of habit. The next morning, they showed up for work at the docks, where they unloaded freshly caught seafood from the boats. The officers were waiting for them, and they promptly arrested the brothers. Wayne and John Carter confessed immediately. They said that they were vampires and that the prostitutes and dock workers they kidnapped were their food source. They needed blood to survive. Each evening at dusk, they removed the bandages from their victims, reopened the wounds on their wrists and drained the blood into cups, which they drank from. A few days after their arrest, Wayne and John Carter were tried as serial killers—not vampires—convicted and executed.

The execution of the Carter brothers was not the end of their story. Locals say that once a year around Mardi Gras, Wayne and John Carter return to their own home. The people who live there now claim to have seen them several times. They said that right after moving into the house, they saw two men standing on the balcony. Convinced that they had trapped two housebreaks in their home, the man and woman walked out to the balcony to confront them. All at once, the two men leaped from the balcony onto the street below and vanished.

THE FEU FOLLET

Gonzales

Ghost lights can be found all over the world. According to *The Encyclopedia of Ghosts and Spirits*, these spectral lights are bluish or blue and yellow flames that either bob or float over the landscape. Some people say they lure travelers off a trail at night in an attempt to get them hopelessly lost. This legend explains why the generic term ignis fatuus (foolish fire) is sometimes used in reference to these strange lights. They are known by a number of different names, such as jack-o'-lanterns, kit-in-the-candlesticks and jenny burnt-tails.

Ghost lights are believed to serve another purpose, as well. In some parts of the world, they are regarded as bad omens, often signifying death. These

The Feu Follet, who were believed to be the souls of unbaptized children, are also known as will-o'-the-wisps. *Wikimedia Commons*.

lights are called will-o'-the-wisps, dead candles and corpse candles. In the United Kingdom, these wandering spirits are called will-o'-the-wykes. They are viewed as evil because of their sinful past. In Germany, these forest spirits, known as the *irrlicht*, follow funeral processions. Swedish folklorists say that these lights are the souls of unbaptized children who roam the countryside, looking for love and acceptance. To Native Americans, these lights are the glowing fingertips of the fire creature or the fire demon. The Danes, however, believe that the lights are a good sign because they tend to appear at the place where treasure has been buried.

The *feu follet* (swamp fairies) are spirits commonly found in French and Louisiana folklore. Some say that the small balls of light are the spirits of souls escaped from purgatory. Others believe that they are the souls of babies who died before they could be blessed by the church. The flitting quality of the lights has led some to conclude that they are fairies dancing in the moonlight.

In many cases, folklore not only reveals the supernatural forces at work in our lives but also prescribes ways to deal with them on a daily basis. Travelers passing through a marshy area by boat at night are advised to head for shore because the feu follet cannot cross water. If a person on foot senses that the feu follet are close behind, the best way to deter them is to stick a knife or knitting needle in the ground.

Of course, a scientific explanation can be given for most of the sightings of these lights. Some people say that they are methane or "swamp gas," The manifestation of "earth energy" has also been offered as an explanation. Others theorize that magnetic or electrical forces are responsible for these spook lights. The folkloric explanations might not be scientific, but they certainly are more stimulating to the imagination.

THE BEAST OF GRUNCH ROAD

New Orleans

New Orleans has a character all of its own. Some of its legends can be found nowhere else in the country. One of these fantastic tales dates back to the city's earliest days when a deformed baby was brought to Voodoo Queen Marie Laveau. She could tell from its evil countenance that it was the spawn of the devil. She castrated the devil baby to prevent it from reproducing.

However, as soon as its testicles fell to the floor, they turned into a male and female Grunch. Aware that Marie Laveau had killed their parent, the creatures bit and beat her, nearly taking her life. When she regained consciousness, her attackers had vanished. Some residents of New Orleans believe that this horrible experience with the Grunch convinced her to turn away from the "dark side" and return to her Catholic beliefs.

Since then, the Grunch has been sighted throughout New Orleans. Witnesses claim to have seen it running around the City Park Golf Course and the levees of the Chalmette National Battlefield. It has also been seen racing across Highway 90 in the Luling, Boutte and Paradis areas. Since Hurricane Katrina, the monster has appeared in the Lakeview area, where it has been mistaken for a raccoon. Legend has it, though, that Grunch Road was its preferred hunting ground. The old road, composed of shells and sand, was located near the community of Little Woods in eastern New Orleans. It snaked its way through the massive water oaks to Hayne Boulevard. Legend has it that at one time a small group of albinos and dwarves lived out there because of its isolated location. It was also a favorite spot for teenagers to party and make out. Many of them reported seeing flashing lights and hearing eerie cries, which they took as evidence of the Grunch's existence. Stories also circulated about the disappearance of curiosity-seekers foolish enough to drive off Hayne Boulevard and search for the monster.

Sightings of the Grunch go back decades. According to reports from New Orleans sanitation workers, the monsters scavenge through garbage cans and have even run after garbage trucks in the Grunch Road area and along East Haynes Boulevard. Witness descriptions of the monster vary, but they share a few common elements. The goat-like beast is said to stand between three and four feet tall. A trail of sharp spines line its back. Some describe its skin as having a leather-like texture; others say it has a black, scaly hide. It is covered with long fur and goat-like markings. The color of its eyes varies, as well, depending on the witness. They have been described as red, orange or blue. The monster possesses the human ability to open doors and use tools. The monster's bloodcurdling howl is said to resemble that of a wolf. Its appearance is always heralded by a nauseating stench.

Cryptozoologists point to the beast's uncanny similarity to the chupacabra, or "goat sucker." First sighted in Puerto Rico, it is reputed to drink the blood of livestock. Like the Grunch, it is a relatively small animal with a row of spines running from its neck to its tail. On the other hand, its goat-like appearance could be said to link it to the devil and to Pan, the Greek god of nature, who was demonized by the Council of Nicaea in 325 AD. Like Pan, the devil is depicted as having horns and the cloven hooves of a goat. To lovers of New Orleans lore, the creature's demonic appearance substantiates the tale that has been told and retold for centuries.

WHO IS THE ROUGAROU?

Houma

Legends of shape-shifting creatures can be found all over the world. Examples include the weretigers of India, the werewolves of France, werejaugars of Mexico and the werehyenas of Africa. The Navajo Indians told tales of skinwalkers, who had the ability to transform into a variety of animals, most notably coyotes. In the twentieth century, physicians deduced that some people who were thought to be suffering from lycanthropy were actually suffering from a genetic disorder called hypertrichosis, which causes hair to grow all over the human body. In parts of Louisiana, however, the belief in one of these supposedly mythical beasts still persists.

The word *Rougarou* is the Cajun variant of the French word *Loup-garou*. Its origin dates back to the medieval period in France, when it was primarily a cautionary tale told to children to prevent them from roaming into the woods alone. In these fanciful stories, the creature had a human body and the head of a wolf. In the early seventeenth century, French immigrants transported their legends along with their possessions to Canada. The French refugees from Acadia (present-day Nova Scotia) brought the loup-garou stories with them to Louisiana in 1765, following their expulsion by the British.

In the Cajun version of the tale, the Rougarou is a red-eyed beast with sharp teeth. It stands between seven and eight feet tall. It is stronger and can run faster than a normal human being. It was said to prowl the swamps, although following Hurricane Katrina, it appears to have expanded its hunting ground to New Orleans. Many of the Catholic residents of Louisiana believed that anyone could become a werewolf. It was also said that the curse could be transferred to anyone who looked into the eyes of a Rougarou. In another variant of the legend, a person who has been a Rougarou for 101 days could be released by transferring the curse to the next person he or she bites. In a less common variant, a witch's curse can transform her victim into a Rougarou.

The Rougarou, which was said to prowl around swampy areas, is the Cajun version of the werewolf. *Wikimedia Commons*.

The prescribed method of killing a Rougarou varies, as well. Some people believe that burning a Rougarou is the best way to dispatch it. Others say that a Rougarou is not really dead until it has been decapitated. Just to be sure that the beast is dead, though, some people go as far as to mutilate the body after it has been beheaded.

Folklore also provides preventative measures for warding off a Rougarou. For years, men placed a leaf in their wallet to ensure that the Rougarou leave them alone wherever they went. Women painted hexagons in the center of the floor of their houses to keep their families safe. For good measure, many offered up prayers.

Many residents of Louisiana take pride in the Rougarou lore, which was an integral part of their ancestors' lives for generations. The legendary beast is celebrated in Houman's annual Rougarou Festival. A Rougarou exhibit can be found in the Audubon Zoo. Supposedly, the New Orleans Pelicans basketball team even considered changing its name to the Rougarous several years ago. For a mythical beast, the Rougarou exerts a very strong hold on the culture of Louisiana.

MISHMASH MONSTERS OF THE MARSHES

Terrebonne Parish

Mythology is populated with human hybrids. In Greek mythology, the centaur possesses the upper body of a human and the lower body of a horse. The harpy has the body of a woman and the legs and wings of a bird. In Roman mythology, the satyr has the upper body of a man and the horns and legs of a goat. In Russian mythology, the *alkonost* has the head of a woman and the body of a bird. Anubis, the Egyptian god of mummification, has the body of a man and the head of a jackal. Sirena in Filipino folklore is a mermaid with the upper torso of a woman and the lower extremities of a fish. Her male counterpart is Slyokoy. In Louisiana lore, a fearsome hybrid called the letiche lurks in the swamps and bayous.

The Cajun legend of the letiche demonstrates the way cultural sharing takes place when different ethnic groups live in proximity. Locals believe that the letiche are the spirits of illegitimate unbaptized children who are condemned to walk the earth as denizens of the swamp, like the feu follet. According to Native American tradition, the leitche are human children who became lost in the swamps and were raised by alligators. Over time, their human traits melded with their reptilian caretaker, creating a murderous hybrid that causes boats to capsize and deposit the passengers into the swamp, where they become easy prey. Many of these legends have been generated around Terrebonne Parish.

Another nightmarish hybrid that is said to inhabit Louisiana's waterways and marshes is the Altmaha-ha. Witnesses describe it as a twenty- to thirty-foot long aquatic creature with the head of an alligator and large, bulging eyes and razor-sharp teeth. Its grayish body resembles that of a sturgeon, with a bony ridge on top. Because it has only front flippers, it is said to swim like a dolphin. Stories of this creature originated around the channels of the Altamaha River in Georgia. Most of the sightings have taken place around the waters of Darien, Georgia, which—it is important to note—was founded by settlers from the shores of Loch Ness in Scotland.

In recent years, sightings of a sea serpent–like creature suggest that Altamaha-ha has migrated to southern Louisiana. In 2014, the Discovery Channel show *Beasts of the Bayou* devoted an entire episode to the Altamaha-ha, affectionately known as "Altie." A member of one of the teams sent to investigate the sightings was Tulane biologist Hank Bart. The group was

Some scientists believe that the Altamaha-ha is actually a giant sturgeon, which also has a bony ridge on top. *animal.memozee.com.*

following up on reports of a monster with an elongated neck and a long, spiny tail. By the end of the expedition, the team found a large manatee but nothing resembling Altie, supporting Bart's original hypothesis that what people have been seeing is nothing more than a giant sturgeon.

THE LUTIN

Louisiana

Trickster figures can be found in belief systems all over the world. As a rule, the trickster is a comparatively small or weak creature that uses its wits to prevail over its physically superior opponents, such as Anansi the spider of African origin. In some folktales, trickster figures are mischievous, playful figures who, by accident or design, inject chaos into the world. By the story's end, they learn a hard lesson from their mistakes, like Coyote in the Native American oral tradition. Generally speaking, trickster tales were instructional narratives told to children in the hope that they would be entertained and educated at the same time.

A classic trickster figure from French folklore that found its way to Louisiana is the Lutin, a hobgoblin-like figure similar to elves, gnomes and leprechauns. In the French fairy tale "Le Prince Lutin," written by Marie Catherin d'Aulnoy in 1697, the Lutin becomes invisible when he dons a red hat with two feathers.

The Lutin figure evolved when the tales were transported to North American by the French, who settled in Quebec. In these stories, the Lutin were shapeshifters who often took the form of domesticated animals, like

Many French immigrants brought with them stories of a trickster figure called the Lutin. *Wikimedia Commons.*

cats. Good-natured Lutins performed useful tasks for the homeowners, like shaving the master's beard or controlling the weather. Bad-natured Lutins acted out in very annoying ways, calculated to attract attention, like filling a shoe with pebbles or blunting farm implements. They were believed to be repelled by salt.

The Cajun version of the Lutin is very similar to its French forebear, with the exception that they are said to be the animated spirits of illegitimate unbaptized children. Their unblessed origin drives these impish creatures to disrupt people's normal routines by spoiling milk and cheese, cutting the hair of sleepers and scaring farm animals. Like poltergeists, the Lutin also delight in moving objects from one place to another. Iron and salt can be used as protection against them. However, these troublesome dwarves are somewhat redeemed by their love of horses. Farmers who walk into the barn and find that their horses' manes and tales have been braided know that they have been paid a visit by the Lutin.

THE HONEY ISLAND SWAMP MONSTER

Slidell

Honey Island Swamp, which is twenty miles long and seven miles across, is considered by wildlife biologists to be one of most pristine swamplands in the entire United States. Approximately half of the swamp's seventy thousand acres constitutes a permanently protected wildlife area. Because so much of the wilderness is practically impenetrable, Honey Island Swamp has become home to a wide variety of wildlife, include alligators, turtles, black bears, nutria, snakes, raccoons, eagles and, some people say, a monster.

The humanoid creature known as Bigfoot or Sasquatch is normally thought to inhabit the northwestern United States. However, the southern varieties of the creature go under several different names, such as skunk ape, swamp cabbage man, and Myakka ape. The best-known example of what has come to be known as the Louisiana Bigfoot is the Honey Island Swamp Monster.

The first reported sighting of the creature took place in 1963. An air traffic controller named Harlan E. Ford was scouring Honey Island Swamp with his hunting buddy, Billy Mills, in search of an abandoned hunting camp. When the men emerged from the woods into a clearing, they were

The mysterious Honey Island Swamp is said to be the home of an anthropoid-like creature that was first sighted by Harlan E. Ford in 1963 while on a hunting trip. *Wikimedia Commons.*

shocked to see a huge animal on all fours. As soon as Billy said, "What is that thing?" the creature stood up on its two hind legs and confronted the interlopers. After a few long seconds, it bounded off into the swamp, leaving nothing but its tracks. When Harlan returned home, he shared his strange encounter with his family. He described the monster as standing seven feet tall with a broad chest and shoulders and slender legs. Long gray strands of hair covered its head, and shorter hairs coated its grayish-colored skin. Its most prominent characteristic, Harlan said, was its large eyes, which were amber in color.

Harlan's next encounter with the monster was even more terrifying. He and Billy returned to the swamp to hunt ducks. They were tromping through a series of muddy sloughs, when they found a wild boar with its throat ripped out. They could tell by the foul odor that it had been killed a day or two before. Warily, the men continued walking, until they found the mutilated carcass of another wild boar. Its throat had been torn out, as well. At first, Harlan thought an alligator might have killed the pigs. On reflection, however, he realized that the boars were too far inland to have been attacked by alligators. Puzzled, they walked on until they approached a pond. Thinking that the ripples in the pond were made by ducks, the men got down on their bellies and were crawling toward the edge of the pond, until they found a third dead boar. It was killed just like the other two. The kill site was covered with large tracks. The stench of the carcass was not very strong, indicating the beast might still be in the area. This time, the men decided to bring back proof of their find. Using the plaster they had brought along, they made casts of several of the prints. Later, Harlan showed the plaster casts to a zoologist at Louisiana State University. The scientist concluded that the tracks were not a hoax. He estimated from the depth of the track in the ground that it weighed approximately four hundred pounds.

The Honey Island Swamp Monster received national attention in 1978, when the television series *In Search Of* devoted an episode to Harland Ford's encounter with the creature. The plaster casts of the four-toed tracks led some to believe that they were the tracks of an alligator. On closer examination, however, a thumblike small toe is visible.

Since Harlan's discovery of the monster, several highly imaginative theories have emerged. Residents who are familiar with the folklore of Louisiana have proposed that the monster could be a letiche. According to Native Americans, the letiche is a human child who was raised by alligators and acquired some of their reptilian features. The hairy appearance of the creature had led some to conclude that the beast is really a Rougarou, a

Some people believe that the strange footprint that Ford preserved in plaster is actually the track of a large alligator. *Wikimedia Commons.*

Descriptions of the Honey Island Swamp Monster match those of Bigfoot, which is called the skunk ape in different parts of the South. *pexels.com*.

Louisiana werewolf. The strangest legend that has been generated by the publicity is that in the early 1900s, a circus train derailed near the Pearl River, not far from Honey Island Swamp. All of the animals that escaped from their cages perished in the swamp, with the exception of a troop of chimpanzees, which interbred with the alligators and produced a bizarre reptilian hybrid that has become known as the Honey Island Monster.

Harlan Ford continued hunting the monster until his death in 1980. Several years after his death, his family discovered Super 8 film footage that he had taken of the monster in Honey Island Swamp. The footage was aired in an episode of the television series *Monsters and Mysteries in America*. The legend continues to be featured on weird America–type television shows Despite the publicity the legend has received, not everyone is a believer. Many of the viewers of the *Monsters and Mysteries* segment believed that the figure in the film might be a camouflaged hunter. Ecologists Paul and Sue Wagner, who operated nature tours in the swamp, dismiss the stories entirely in the absence of hard evidence. Of course, there are some people who believe that the legends might have been fabricated to keep would-be hunters out of the area.

WORKS CITED

Books

Brown, Alan. *Haunted Places in the American South*. Jackson: University Press of Mississippi, 2002.

Brown, Ethan. *Murder on the Bayou*. New York: Scribner, 2016.

Butler, Anne Butler. *The Pelican Guide to Plantation Homes of Louisiana*. Gretna, LA: Pelican Publishing, 2013.

Cassady, Charles, Jr. *Crescent City Crimes*. Atglen, PA: Schiffer Publishing 2017.

Crandle, Marita Woywod. *New Orleans Vampires: History and Legend*. Charleston, SC: The History Press 2017.

Davis, Miriam C. *The Axeman of New Orleans: The True Story*. Chicago: Chicago Review Press, 2017.

Dwyer, Jeff. *Ghost Hunter's Guide to New Orleans*. Gretna, LA: Pelican Publishing, 2007.

Fortier, Alcee. *Compare Lapin and Piti Bonhomme Godron (The Tar Baby)*. N.p.: Zoe Company, 1996.

Guiley, Rosemary. *The Encyclopedia of Ghosts and Spirits*. New York: Checkmark Books, 2000.

Jameson, W.C. Jameson. *Buried Treasure of the South: Legends of Lost, Buried, and Forgotten Treasures—From Tidewater Virginia and Coastal Carolina to Cajun Louisiana*. Little Rock, AR: August House Publishers, 1992.

Klein, Victor C. *New Orleans Ghosts*. Chapel Hill, NC: Professional Press, 1993.

LeJune, Keagan. *Always the Underdog: Leather Britches Smith and the Grabow War*. Denton: University of North Texas Press, 2010.

Norman, Michael, and Beth Scott. *Haunted America*. New York: Tor, 1994.

Ramsay, Jack C. *Jean Lafitte: Prince of Pirates*. New York: Eakins Press, 1996.

Sammonda, Mary Beth, and Robert Edwards. *American Hauntings*. New York: Barnes & Noble, 2005.

Saxon, Lyle, Edward Dreyer and Robert Tallant. *Gumbo Ya-Ya*. Gretna, LA: Pelican Publishing, 1987.

Stuart, Bonnye. *Haunted New Orleans*. Guilford, CT: Globe Pequot Press, 2012.

Taylor, Troy. *Haunted New Orleans*. Alton, IL: White Chapel Press, 2000.

Turnage, Sheila. *Haunted Inns of the Southeast*. Salem, NC: John F. Blair: 2001.

Wilton, David. *Word Myths: Debunking Linguistic Urban Legends*. Oxford, UK: Oxford University Press, 2008.

Internet Articles

Baram, Marcus. "A Grisly New Orleans Murder Mystery Takes Another Twist." October 24, 2006. ABC. https://abcnews.go.com.

Bartlette, DeLani R. "The Gruesome Tale of Zack Bowen and Addie Hall—And What It Says About Our Fascination with True Crime." Medium, April 29, 2019. https://medium.com.

Bennett, Tara. "Haunted History." Baton Rouge Dig, October 28, 2014. https://digbr.com.

"'Birthplace of Dixie' Plaque." Atlas Obscura. https://www.atlasobscura.com.

"Bobby Dunbar: The Boy Who Vanished and Came Back as a New Child." All That's Interesting. Allthats interesting.com.

Bourbon Orleans Hotel. "A Haunted New Orleans Hotel." https://www.bourbonorleans.com.

Boyd, Andrew. "St. Louis Cemetery No. 1: Is Marie Laveau Where They Say She Is?" *Times-Picayune*, May 22, 2018. https://nola.com.

Branley, Edward. "History of the Casket Girls of New Orleans." Go Nola, October 16, 2018. https://gonola.com.

BREC. "Frenchtown Road Conservation Area." www.brec.org.

Clodfelter, Tim. "Ask Sam: Where Did the Word 'Dixie' Come From?" *Winston-Salem Journal*. https://www.journalnow.com.

"Confederate Submarine Base Located." *American Civil War Society Newsletter* (Spring 2015) https://acws.col.uk.

"Court of the Two Sisters—New Orleans, LA (An Eternal Sisterly Bond)." *Haunted Nation* (blog). http://hauntednation.blogspot.com.

Court of Two Sisters. "Our History." https://www.courtoftwosisters.com.

Crandle, Marita. "A Vampire in New Orleans? The Mysterious Case of Jacque and the Comte de St. Germain." Ancient Origins, October 23, 2017. Ancientorigins.net.

Cryptid Wiki. "Honey Island Swamp Monster." https://cryptidz.fandom.com.

Davis, Miriam. "The Axeman of New Orleans Preyed on Italian Immigrants." *Smithsonian Magazine*, February 15, 2018. https://www.smithsonianmag.com.

"The Day the War Stopped." *Friends in St. Francisville, LA* (blog). Stfrancisville.blogspot.com.

Eden, Cynthia. "Monster Lights from Louisiana." Cynthia Eden. https://cynthiaeden.com.

Explore Southern History. "Altamaha-ha—Sea Monster of the Georgia Coast." https://www.exploresouthernhistory.com.

Fold3. "Yoakum, Yocum, Yocom." https://www.fold3.com.

Gage, Joan. "Nicolas Cage & the LaLaurie House Curse." *A Rolling Crone* (blog), November 19, 2009. Arollingcronblogspot.com.

Ghost City Tours. "The Haunted Bourbon Orleans Hotel." https://ghostcitytours.com.

———. "Marie Laveau, the Voodoo Queen of New Orleans." https://ghostcitytours.com.

"Gold Coins Found in Honey Island Swamp." *Tammany Family* (blog). https://tammanyfamily.blogspot.com.

Graves, Kandace Power. "Where Exactly in City Park Are the Dueling Oaks and the Suicide Oak?" Gambit, February 8, 2016. https://www.nola.com.

Hancock County Historical Society. "Alphabet File Page 263." hancockcountyhistoricalsociety.com.

Harvey, Ian. "Local Shreveport Man Believes He Found Lost Confederate Submarines." *Vintage News* (blog), April 5, 2016. https://www.thevintagenews.com.

Haunted Houses. "T-Freres House and Garconniere." https://ghost.hauntedhouses.com.

"Haunted Louisiana—The Old State Capitol Building." *Author Lyn Gibson* (blog), October 9, 2016. Authorlyngibson.wordpress.com.

Haunted New Orleans Tours. "Was It When People Started Disappearing Down Grunch Road That Everyone Finally Took Notice?" www.hauntedneworleanstours.com.

Haunted Places. "Diamond Grill." hauntedplaces.org.

———. "Harris Hall—University of Louisiana at Lafayette." https://www.hauntedplaces.org.

Haunted Places to Go. "The Haunted Oak Alley Plantation." https://www.haunted-places-to-go.com.

Haunted Rooms. "The Most Haunted Places in Louisiana." https://www.hauntedrooms.com.

Haunt LA. "Ellerbe Road School." http://hauntla.com.

Horsfall, Ashley. "Who Murdered Eight Women in Jennings?" Medium. https://medium.com.

Hotel Bentley. "The Hotel Bentley Since 1908." www.visithotelbentley.com.

Houmas House. "Houmas House." houmashouse.com.

Houston Chronicle. "Ghost Stories of the Past at Louisiana Plantation." https://www.Chron.com.

"Jesse Ray Yocum and the Murrell Gang." *Remembering the Shoals* (blog). https://rememberingtheshoals.wordpress.com.

Kincaid, Ezekiel. "The Tetromet Chronicles." *Ezekiel Kincaid* (blog). https://ezekielkincaid.wordpress.com.

KLFY. "Haunted in Acadiana—T'Frere's Bed & Breakfast." klfy.com.

K95. "Northwest Louisiana Haunted Tales: Ellerbe Road School." https://k945.com.

Kplctv. "Haunted SWLA: The Beauregard Parish Hanging Jail." www.kplctv.com.

———. "Is the Hanging Jail in DeRidder Really Haunted?" www.kplctv.com.

KTBS. "The Urban Legends of Ellerbe Road School." https://www.ktbs.com.

Kunesh, Tom. "Sickness and Death in the Old South: Facing East, the Traditional Burial Position." Tennessee Project. https://www.tngenweb.org.

Legends of America.com. "The Axeman of New Orleans." https://www.legendsofamerica.com.

Le Monroe, H. "Unsolved: The Axeman of New Orleans." Medium. https://medium.com.

Little Things Travel. "New Orleans Voodoo: Triple X Marks the Spot." https://www.littlethingstravel.com

Louisiana Digital Library. "The King of Honey Island." https://louisianadigitallibrary.org.

"Louisiana Ghost Stories: Le Lutin." *Red Housewife* (blog). theredhousewife.blogspot.com.

Louisiana Haunted Houses. "Shreveport Municipal Memorial Auditorium—Shreveport LA Real Haunt." Louisianahauntedhouses.com.

Louisiana Myths and Legends. "Leather Britches Smith." https://www.louisianamythsandlegends.com.

Lovejoy, Bess. "The Legend (and Truth) of the Voodoo Preistess Who Haunts a Louisiana Swamp." Mental Floss, October 14, 2017. https://www.mentalfloss.com.

"Lutin." *Demoniacal* (blog). thedemoniacal.blogspot.com.

Mann, Marilu. "A Louisiana Ghost Story: Le Feu Follet." *Marilu Mann* (blog). Marilumannbooks.com.

Men's Health. "Here's the True Story of How Bonnie and Clyde Died." menshealth.com.

Mesa Community College. "The Demonization of Pan." mesacc.edu.

Michael, Jay. "Honey Island Swamp Monster." http://jmichaelms.tripod.com.

Mimsy Were the Borogoves. "Mimsy Review: The Legend of the Nightriders." https://www.hoboes.com.

Mississippi Encyclopedia. "John Murrell." https://mississippiencyclopedia.org.

Modern Farmer. "When Animals Fall from the Sky." https://modernfarmer.com.

MUFON "Louisiana Witness Captures Triangle UFO on Video." https://www.mufon.com.

National Park Service. "Laura Plantation." http://www.cr.nps.gov.

———. "Parlange Plantation House." http://www.cr.nps.gov.

Navsource. "Pioneer & Pioneer II." www.navsource.org.

New Orleans Bar. "Fort de la Boulaye Was First." neworleansbar.org.

New Orleans City Park. "Live Oaks of City Park." neworleanscitypark.com.

"Nightriders: West-Kimbrell Gang." www.jcs-group.com.

Oak Alley Plantation. "Legends, Lore & Sprits—The Shadows of Oak Alley." www.oakalleyplantation.org.

Only in Your State. "Houma Tunnel Is a Haunted Tunnel in Louisiana That Has a Dark History." https://www.onlyinyourstate.com.

People pill. "John Murrell (bandit)." https://peoplepill.com.

Reddit. "The 1991 Disappearance of A.J. Breaux: Recovering Alcoholic Vanishes While Driving Home from A.A. Meeting." https://www.reddit.co.

Shayne, Tasha. "Mysterious Booms Heard Around the World Leaving People Perplexed." Gaia, July 10, 2019. https://www.gaia.com.

Shelton, Beth B. "The Mystery of the Silver Bell." Medium. https://medium.com.

Soltis, Andy. "Gal-Cooker in an 11 Day 'Stew' Por-Confessed in Suicide Note." *New York Post.* https://nypost.com.

Southern Spirit Guide. "Shreveport Municipal Memorial Auditorium." southernspiritguide.org.

"Spanish Moon—Baton Rouge, LA (Spirits of All Kinds)." *Haunted Nation* (blog). http://hauntednation.blogspot.com.

Stephen F. Austin State University. "The Grave of the Unknown Confederate Soldier (March 2012)." www.stasu.edu.

———. "John Murrell's Hideouts (April 2019)." www.sfasu.edu.

"Travel Channel Episode Features Marksville's 1947 'Rain of Fish.'" *Avoyelles Today.* https://archive.avoyellestoday.com.

Try to Scare Me. "Carter Brothers: New Orleans. LA." Trytoscareme.com.

UFO Insight. "The Louisiana Sightings—UFOs in the American Deep South." Ufosight.com.

United States Naval Academy. "The Day the War Stopped." https://www.usna.edu.

Unsolved Mysteries Wiki. "A.J. Breaux." https://unsolvedmysteries.fandom.com.

———. "Eric and Pam Ellender." https://unsolvedmysteries.fandom.com.

———. "Hazel Head." https://unsolvedmysteries.fandom.com.

———. "Thomas Hotard and Audrey Moate." https://unsolvedmysteries.fandom.com.

USS *Kidd*. "Ship History: Explore the Kidd." usskidd.com.

Vanity Fair. "Nicolas Cage Says the Best Night of His Life Involved a Full Moon and His Father's Ashes." https://wanityfair.com.

Vermillion. "Skeptics and Believers Respond to Alleged Louisiana UFO Sighting." http://www.thevermillion.com.

———. "University Officials Tight-Lipped About Harris Hall Ghost Tale, Suspected Nightly Hauntings." http://www.thevermillion.com.

Vertigo. "The Phantom Whistler of Louisiana." https://www.vertigo.22.com.

Vining, Season. "Legend Has It: Urban Legends of the Bayou." Baton Rouge Dig, September 30, 2017. https://digbr.com.

Week in Weird.com. "The Curse of Julia Brown: Manchac Swamp's Voodoo Priestess Haunts Louisiana After Killing a Whole Town." http://weekinweird.com.

"What Is a Rougarou, Exactly?" *Cryptoville* (blog). https://visitcryptoville.com.

"Women Wanted in Boyfriends' Murders." Fox News.

"Wrong Way Cemetery." Atlas Obscura, December 23, 2019. https://www.atlasobscura.com.

Wyatt, Megan. "I Stayed at a 'Haunted' Acadiana B&B." *Daily Advertiser*, October 14, 2015.

Magazines and Journals

Bass, Erin Z. "City of Spirits." *Deep South Magazine*, October 25, 2018.

Drell, Cady. "Dark Truth Behind 8 Sex Workers Murdered in the Bayou." *Rolling Stone*, September 27, 2016.

"Flolklore Scrap-Book: Lutins in the Province of Quebec." *Journal of American Folklore* 5, no. 19 (December 1892): 327–28.

Leger, Benjamin. "A Look at Some of Baton Rouge's Most Haunted Locations." *225 Magazine*, October 3, 2018. https://www.225batonrouge.com.

Rivers, William L. "Looking for Louisiana's Lost Loot." *Modern Mechanix*, March 1956.